DEPARTMENT OF TRANSPORT

RAILWAY ACCIDENT

Report on the Collapse of Glanrhyd Bridge on 19th October 1987

IN THE

WESTERN REGION

OF BRITISH RAILWAYS

LONDON: HMSO

ISBN 0 11 550961 5

RAILWAY INSPECTORATE
DEPARTMENT OF TRANSPORT
2 MARSHAM STREET
LONDON SW1P 3EB

31st January 1990

SIR,

I report for the information of the Secretary of State for Transport, in accordance with the Direction dated 16 November 1987, the result of my Inquiry into the accident to a passenger train which occurred on 19 October 1987 at Glanrhyd between Llandeilo and Llandovery in the Western Region of British Railways.

At approximately 07.15 on the Monday morning a Swansea to Shrewsbury passenger train consisting of a two-car diesel-multiple-unit (DMU) ran onto the bridge carrying the Central Wales railway over the River Towy at Glanrhyd. Following many hours of heavy rainfall the Towy valley was extensively flooded and during the hours of darkness the bridge had collapsed into the river. The train stopped with the rear coach on part of the bridge which remained above water but the leading coach landed in the swollen and fast flowing river.

Of the ten persons travelling on the train three passengers and three members of British Railways' staff were able to escape but I regret to report that three passengers (Mr and Mrs W B Evans and Simon Penny) and the driver of the train (Mr J M Churchill) were drowned.

The bridge was damaged beyond repair and it had to be completely demolished. The service was maintained over the Central Wales Line by the means of a connecting bus service between Llandeilo and Llandovery Stations until the bridge was reconstructed. A single span steel girder bridge on new foundations was erected and the line re-opened to rail services on 30 October 1988.

DESCRIPTION

The Line and its Signalling

1.   The bridge over the River Towy at Glanrhyd carries the Central Wales Line between Llandeilo and Llangadog Stations. The Central Wales Line runs from Llanelli in the south to Craven Arms in the north where it joins the Hereford to Shrewsbury line. The line was built in stages by different railway companies between 1835 and 1868. The line between Llandeilo and Llandovery was constructed by the Vale of Towy Railway Company and was opened to traffic in 1858.

2.   The Central Wales Line is predominantly a single line railway with passing loops at Pantyffynon, Llandeilo, Llandovery, Llanwrtyd and Llandrindod Wells. The signalling of trains over the line between Pantyffynon and Craven Arms is by an electric key token system known as 'No Signalman Token with Remote Loops' (NSTR). It is supervised by a signalman at Pantyffynon but the token exchange equipment at the passing loops is operated by the train crew.

3.   Mileage of the Central Wales Line is taken from the Llanelli end of the line. The bridge over the River Towy at Glanrhyd is close to the 22½ mile post. The line is depicted at Diagram 1.

The Train

4.   The train involved in the accident was the 05.27 passenger train, 2M31, from Swansea to Shrewsbury on Monday 19 October 1987. The first part of the train's journey was over the Swansea to Carmarthen main line as far as Llanelli where the direction of travel of the train reversed. The train was timetabled to depart from Llanelli at 05.46 and to arrive at Shrewsbury at 09.17. The train was formed of a two car DMU. The reversal of direction at Llanelli resulted in the car which was the leading one on the departure from Swansea being the trailing car on the journey over the Central Wales Line. In this report references are to leading and trailing cars after the train departed from Llanelli.

5.   The leading car was a Class 108 driving motor second No. 52037. It had a driving cab across the full width of the outer end of the vehicle. There was a vestibule connection to the trailing car at its inner end. The car, which was built in 1960, was 17.70m long and weighed 28.5 tonnes. Internally, the passenger accommodation was divided into three sections. Immediately behind the driving cab was a section of 12 seats previously provided for First Class passengers. The centre section contained 33 and the rear section 20 Standard Class seats. A lavatory was also provided at the rear of the car.

6.   The driving cab had outward opening doors on each side. It was separated from the former First Class section by a partition the upper part of which was glass. In this partition was a sliding door allowing staff to move between the driving cab and the passenger compartment. Between the front and middle, and middle and rear passenger compartments there were transverse lobbies leading to outward opening passenger doors on each side of the car. The former First Class compartment was separated from the front lobby by a partition, the upper part of which was glass. This partition contained a sliding door. The other seating was separated from the lobbies by similar partitions but with openings without doors. There was a sliding door at the rear of the car across the gangway connection.

7.   The trailing car was a similar vehicle but was a driving motor brake second. The inner (leading) section of the car was a brake van. The centre and trailing sections of the car consisted of Standard Class seating. There was a full width driving cab at the rear of the car. The layout of the DMU is depicted in Diagram 2.

The Bridge
8.   A survey of the bridge in 1949 and photographs taken in 1957 show a single track bridge with 5 spans comprising deck timbers resting on pairs of wrought iron box girders. These were supported from masonry bank seat abutments and by 4 intermediate masonry piers. No details of the foundations were shown. Because the wrought iron girders were overstressed, the superstructure of the bridge was reconstructed in 1958.

9.   The new steel superstructure was a 5-span 'Half through bridge' of welded plate main girders and welded prefabricated standard steel deck units which were waterproofed and tiled. A steel public footbridge was cantilevered from the downstream main girders. The bridge soffit level was raised by 840 mm as previously flood water had reached the level of the timber decking. The raising of the soffit level was achieved by casting concrete blocks on top of the existing abutments and piers.

10.   The bridge spans, numbered 1 to 5 from the 'Swansea end', were simply supported and approximately 50 ft., 56 ft., 56 ft., 56 ft. and 49 ft. in length respectively. The masonry piers which supported the steel work were also numbered from the Swansea end. Pier 1 was at the Swansea edge of the main watercourse. Pier 2 was in the centre of the main watercourse at approximately the deepest part. Piers 3 and 4 were located out of the main watercourse on the flood plane. The general arrangement of the bridge is shown in Diagram 3.

11.   The bridge was at a 46° angle of skew and the girders were articulated over the piers to eliminate asymmetrical loading on the piers. Loads were transferred from the girders to the piers via steel bearing blocks and baseplates on the concrete blocks. The prefabricated deck units were connected at the end of each cross girder by 12 bolts to the 'T' stiffeners. Adjacent deck units were interconnected to intermediate trough units by 20 bolts. Longitudinal movement of the bridge was restrained by transverse bearing keep plates on piers 2 and 3. Transverse movement of the bridge was restrained by longitudinal bearing keep plates on all the piers and the abutment.

EVIDENCE

As to events on Sunday 18 October
12.   *Mr A Scott*, a British Railways Traffic Manager, was on Sunday 18 October the 'On-call' operating manager for the Swansea area including the Central Wales Line. On the Sunday morning he had been working in the Margam area where his normal post was. He had returned home from there about halfpast two in the afternoon. About 10 o'clock in the evening, he was at home when he received a telephone call from the signalman at Pantyffynon.

13.   He was advised by the signalman that the driver of a 'light' locomotive, which was returning from engineering work in the Llandrindod Wells area, had reported that there was flooding of the track. Three specific areas were mentioned and there was reference to ballast being washed away. The signalman said that he had already called out a member of the permanent way staff to examine the line. He also told Mr Scott that he was closing the signal box at midnight but would be returning to duty at five o'clock the following morning. Mr Scott said that the signalman was concerned that he should be told the result of any inspection that took place while the signal box was closed.

14.   Mr Scott telephoned the supervisor at Swansea High Street, who was responsible for the operation of all the passenger trains in the Swansea and West Wales area. He explained to the supervisor that there

had been some reports of flooding and that this could possibly have an effect on the morning train service. He had said that it was possible that the 5.27 Swansea to Shrewsbury train might have to be held back or used to examine the line. The supervisor told him of some similar problems in the Fishguard area where the track had been damaged and that engineers had gone there to rectify the problem.

15. After the telephone conversation with the supervisor, Mr Scott decided to take his car and drive towards Llandeilo to investigate the situation for himself. He said he went by the Cross Hands road and there was a small patch of flooding between there and Llandeilo until he got to the road bridge just north of Ffairfach. There it appeared that the river had only just burst its banks and after discussing the situation with a Police Officer, who was nearby, he drove through the water and onto Llandeilo.

16. He parked his car actually on the platform at Llandeilo station where he met a former member of railway staff and they discussed the weather conditions. The other man was a bit concerned that he might not be able to get to work in the morning because he knew the road to Ferryside was flooded. He then telephoned the supervisor again and explained to him that the water had been across the road. In the meantime the operating supervisor had heard from the permanent way supervisor, who it appeared, had tried to get north from Ammanford but had turned back at the same flood water Mr Scott had driven through.

17. Mr Scott then decided to try to get further along the road towards Llandovery but not far along the road where there is a flat area the road was flooded. There was a Woman Police Officer there and after discussions with her and trying to walk through the water, he decided it was unwise to go any further by car and that it would be better to go back to the south of Llandeilo and the flood water to avoid being cut off himself.

18. Mr Scott drove back to the south of the floodwater and then decided to try to look at the railway between Ffairfach and Llandeilo. He walked down a side road and climbed up a bridge abutment to get onto the railway. He walked north along the railway line; it was dark and he said that he could hear the sound of water all around. Surprisingly, he met a man walking a dog along the line who had used a bridge to the south of Llandeilo to cross the river.

19. Mr Scott made his way onto this bridge and looked down at the water. There was some scaffolding on the upstream side of the bridge and this appeared to be causing some damming effect to the water. He walked further north towards Llandeilo station the lights of which he could see but knowing one of the areas reported as being flooded was some six miles away he decided that it would be foolish to try to walk so far in darkness on his own.

20. He decided that the best thing to do was to go home, get some rest and then in the morning accompany the 5.27 Swansea to Shrewsbury train to examine the line. He arrived home at about one o'clock and again spoke by telephone with the supervisor at Swansea and confirmed to him that in the morning he would be driving to Pantyffynon to join the Shrewsbury train. Mr Scott wanted the supervisor to know so that he could advise the Pantyffynon signalman when he booked on in the morning. At about half past one the supervisor at Carmarthen telephoned to tell him that because of serious flooding he was having to abandon the station there. He telephoned the Regional Control Office at Swindon to report to them the Carmarthen situation and then set off to drive there.

21. He was unable to get into Carmarthen because of the flooding but eventually he reached Carmarthen Junction Signal Box. There was a message waiting for him at the signal box to say that Mr Ray Davies, the Permanent Way Supervisor at Llandrindod Wells, was trying to contact him. He telephoned Mr Davies from a public telephone box and was told that a member of the permanent way staff had been unable to get north of Ffairfach-Llandeilo because of the flooding. Mr Scott told him he wanted to examine the line in the morning with the 5.27 train and Mr Davies agreed to try to get south to Llandeilo to meet the train.

22. At about half past three Mr Scott was able to get to Carmarthen Station and he started to make arrangements for the following day's train services. He realised that he was going to be busily employed at Carmarthen and so he telephoned Mr Sharpe, who was the second 'on-call' man. He told Mr Sharpe about the report of flooding on the Central Wales Line and suggested he went to Swansea and either accompanied the 5.27 train or arranged for a member of the permanent way staff to do so.

23. *Mr J C Andrews, the Permanent Way Planning Assistant* for the British Railways' Area Civil Engineer, Swansea, was the 'On-call' Engineer over the week-end of the accident. He told me that he was contacted on the Saturday evening about the late arrival of staff at Craven Arms. During the Sunday

3

morning he was advised by the Permanent Way Section Supervisor (PWSS) at Haverfordwest that following heavy rain in the Fishguard area some ballast had been washed away from the side of the track. After discussion with the PWSS and also with the Operating Supervisor at Swansea it was decided that the boat train could be run and the Regional Control at Swindon was informed.

24. He told me that he had received no warnings of serious flooding of the Central Wales Line. He had not received any notification of concern about bridges anywhere in the area. Mr Andrews said he believed that all departments were aware that anything affecting the Civil Engineer's Department should be routed through the 'on-call' engineer.

25. The driver of the 'light' locomotive was *Relief Driver E J Rossiter*. He explained that having stabled an engineer's train at Craven Arms he was driving the locomotive back to Pantyffynon. He said the journey was trouble-free until Llandovery. Having exchanged single line tokens there he departed towards Llandeilo. At approximately the 26 mile post, which is between Llandovery and Llanwrda, there was some flooding of the track but the water was not above rail level.

26. At about 21.15 he stopped the locomotive briefly on the bridge at Glanrhyd to watch the river. He looked out on the downstream side of the bridge and estimated the water level was three feet below the bridge. Although it was dark and raining he could see the reflection of the water. He continued the journey towards Llandeilo and at approximately the 21 mile post there was further flooding and some of the stone ballast had been displaced from beneath the track. From there towards Llandeilo he drove the locomotive at a very slow speed because he was unsure what to expect. At the 18½ mile post just outside Llandeilo flood water was running above the level of the rails and he drove the locomotive slowly through it at about 3 mile/h.

27. On arriving at Llandeilo he telephoned the signalman at Pantyffynon and reported the three areas of flooding to him. Part way through making his report the signalman asked him to wait while he got a pencil and paper so he could write it down. Mr Rossiter said he particularly mentioned his concern about the displacement of ballast and the water being above the rails at the 18½ mile post.

28. He told me he had been based at Pantyffynon since February 1987 but previously had been based there for some nine and a half years. He said he had never, in the time he had travelled over the line, seen conditions like they were that night, but he had no reservations about driving the locomotive onto the Glanrhyd or any of the other bridges.

29. The signalman, who had been on duty at Pantyffynon Signal Box on Sunday and again on the Monday morning, was *Mr D L M Bowen*. He finished duty at 22.35 on the Sunday night and recommenced at 05.30 on the Monday morning. He had been a signalman at Pantyffynon for eight years.

30. He confirmed that on the Sunday evening he received a telephone call from the driver of a 'light' locomotive returning from Craven Arms to Pantyffynon. The driver reported that there was flooding at the 26, 21 and 18½ mile posts. He said, however, that he could not remember the exact details of what had been said. He telephoned Mr Davies at home and told him that the line was flooded and the ballast washed away in various places. The telephone call from the driver was automatically recorded but the telephone call to Mr Davies was not.

As to events on Monday 19 October

31. Mr Bowen told me that when he opened the signal box on the Monday morning the telephone was ringing. It was Mr Davies, who was at Llandovery, to say that he could not get through by road to Llandeilo but he would try again. Mr Davies telephoned again to say that he had stopped a lorry and was going to travel on it to Llandeilo; later he telephoned from Llandeilo to say he had arrived.

32. Mr Davies said that he would examine the line with the passenger train and when he came to the flooded parts he would get out and check the track. Mr Bowen said he had confirmed with Mr Davies that it would be in order to return the train to Llandeilo if the flooding was too bad. In the meantime Mr Sharpe had telephoned him from Swansea and told him to hold the train at Pantyffynon until he got there. In due course Mr Sharpe arrived and the train departed for Llandeilo. At 07.05 the driver was given the token to proceed from Llandeilo to Llandovery to examine the line. The Control Office informed Mr Bowen at 07.50 that the train was stopped at Glanrhyd bridge and then at about 08.00 it was derailed on the bridge.

33.   I asked Mr Bowen specifically about the regulations, which were laid down for permitting a train to enter a section of line when the line was to be examined. He told me it was permissible to use a passenger train to examine the line providing it was not foggy or snowing. I also asked him about the instructions to be given to the train driver and he told me that there was a form of words which should be used. He said that he could not remember if he had used the correct form of words on that occasion.

34.   *Mr Carwyn Davies* with his father farms land which is alongside the river and the railway line. On the morning of the accident they had got up for milking at the usual time of about quarter past six and as they were crossing the yard they heard a cow bellowing from a field. The floodwater from the river was up to the farm house and he decided to wait for daylight before going to investigate.

35.   Shortly after seven o'clock with daylight just coming in he made his way across the road and into the fields alongside a fence. He said that he was up to his waist in water and the water was flowing too strongly for him to walk through it without hanging onto the fence. He was in the same field as the bridge but the closest he was able to get to it was some 400 yards.

36.   He told me that when he looked towards the bridge, which normally looked quite high when viewed from the field, it "had gone". Although it was still quite dark and raining he could see the bridge against the lighter background. He said that there was a piece of the bridge at each side but he could see a 'V' shape in the middle of the bridge.

37.   Before he was able to return to the farm to telephone he heard a train approaching. He hurried through the water towards the house and got within about 50 yards of it, some 500 to 600 yards from the bridge, when he saw the train crash into the river. He said the first carriage appeared to take off when it reached the collapsed part of the bridge and landed on the other side. It went out of sight into the water and then came back up and floated. He then made his way back to the house and telephoned the police.

38.   He said he was able to see the train for some 150 yards before the bridge and it was travelling slower than normal but somewhat faster than walking pace. He estimated that the front coach remained above the water for some 20 minutes but by the time the police arrived it had turned away from the other carriage and gone underwater.

39.   Mr Davies told me that it was not unusual for the area to be flooded. There had been six floods in the previous winter but he said that this one was the highest he had experienced. After the police arrived they had attempted to get to the bridge using a tractor but it was not possible. He said that in every flood trees would be washed down the river but he had not noticed any tree trunks by the bridge that morning.

40.   *Mr R B Borgiani* was a passenger on the train from Swansea and was intending to travel to Llandovery. He was travelling in the front coach with five or six other passengers as the train approached the bridge. He said he thought the journey from Swansea was a normal one but it was a very wet morning and it was raining a lot.

41.   He told me there was a very loud noise and the train went down. A door on the right opened and a woman in front of him fell down. He said that there was a lot of water coming into the coach from the windows and around the door on the left hand side. He could see the river half way up the windows. He tried to climb out of the coach and onto the roof but could not. He was then told by a railwayman, he believed to be Mr Sharpe, to go into the back coach.

42.   He said the water in the front coach was about one metre deep and that water was coming in between the two coaches. It was difficult, he said, to get through from one coach to the other because they were at an angle.

43.   *Mr K W Bailey* joined the train as a passenger at Llandeilo at "just after seven o'clock". He told me that he had joined the train with Mr Davies, one of the railway engineers. He said he went to sit down in the front coach and that as he was settling himself the train stopped. He looked out of the window and saw water was lapping on the sleepers but it was not on the rails. He said that he saw a man with a torch and he had presumed he was going along the track to look at it.

44.   After about three or four minutes the train started and moved on for about 500 yards before stopping again for about two minutes. When the train moved off it picked up speed until it was travelling at between 30 and 40 mile/h. When he looked through the window he could see that the track was clear of water but the fields alongside the track were flooded. About a mile further on the train slowed down to what Mr Bailey estimated was between 15 and 20 mile/h.

5

45.   He said that all of a sudden there was "this terrific bang, like a crack". There was a blue flash, the lights started to spark and then went out leaving the coach in darkness. Then the water started to come in from the front of the train which had dipped downwards. Having been thrown forward the inrush of water covered Mr Bailey's head. He managed to get up through the dislodged seat cushions and then stood on a seat while he wondered what to do next.

46.   He told me it was just beginning to come light and that he could see the water rising slightly outside the train. He decided to move and paddled and swam towards the back of the train using the luggage racks to steady himself. The water was up to the top of his chest. When he reached the connection between the two coaches he was not sure whether the water was coming in or rushing out from there. He described it as being like rapids and said there was an awful noise.

47.   He found it very difficult to get through the connection. As he was doing so the coach started to shake and the connection seemed to be closing in. He could not remember if Mrs Angus was in front of him at that stage but he thought he had pushed her through. He heard the guard shouting "come this way, it's safer". The rear coach was at an angle and, although it was wet, water was not coming in. He was able to make his way to the rear of the coach and out of an open door onto a girder of the bridge. He stood there for a few seconds and then he saw Mrs Angus and Mr Borgiani. They walked down the track to the station house.

48.   *Mrs A B Angus* was intending that morning to travel to Manchester on business and had originally planned to go to Llandeilo station. She decided because of the reports of flooding overnight to go to Llandybie. The train was late and she did not expect that it would come because "the conditions were appalling". She recalled hearing the church clock strike a quarter to seven, and between 5 and 10 minutes afterwards the train arrived. She noticed another person, who she later learnt was Mr Borgiani, in the front coach she boarded.

49.   She told me that the train journey to Llandeilo was normal but the water was close to the bottom of the steel bridge which carries the line over the River Towy. While the guard was making out an additional ticket for her journey from Llandybie to Llandeilo she asked him if the train would still make the connection with their next train at Shrewsbury. She told me that he said that it would be decided at Llandeilo if the train would continue.

50.   After the train departed from Llandeilo it stopped again just north of the station and a man in a yellow waterproof suit got on and went into the driver's cab. She now knew the man to be Mr Davies. She said the train then departed at normal speed. When it came to that part of the line where the river flows close to the right hand side of the track she saw the river was a "raging torrent". She told me that there was water on both sides and Mr and Mrs Evans and herself had risen from their seats and that "we were terrified". She said that they spoke about their fears, because they had never seen flooding like it before with the water running so very fast.

51.   In order to distract herself from her apprehension she began to read a book. Mrs Angus estimated the speed of the train at 60 mile/h. She said the train slowed once, or perhaps twice in the next few miles to a speed that she found harder to estimate. The last speed she remembered before the crash seemed to be about 25 mile/h but she said she could be wrong by about 10 mile/h. Thinking about it afterwards she estimated the speed was about three times walking speed.

52.   Mrs Angus said she heard a muffled bang and, simultaneously, the carriage she was in began to point downward and, at the same time, water began sweeping back and rising up the carriage. She was thrown out of her seat and into the partition, which divided the passenger compartment, bumping her head. The water went over her head and she tried to swim upwards to get out of it.

53.   She told me that "we all stood there stunned - that is all I can say - for quite a while" and "time is difficult". "It seemed like half an hour, but of course, it wasn't half an hour". At that stage she thought that the rear carriage was also stranded in the river. She said there was no way to know that the rear carriage was out of the water and, because water was rushing between the two carriages, it seemed like the water level was higher to the rear. After what Mrs Angus thought was about 5 minutes she heard a voice say "come back" but, because her instinct was still telling her not to go where the water was higher, she did not.

54.   A person, who she thought was the guard, came into the carriage from the rear and then went back again. She said she again heard the call to come back and thought that this was about 10 minutes

after the crash. Mrs Angus thought the water was a little deeper and there were loose seats and other debris floating in the water. She half walked and half swam to the rear of the carriage.

55.　When she got to the connection between the two carriages it was "quite hard to get across there" and the guard and Mr Bailey helped her through the narrow opening and into the rear carriage. She said she was astonished to find that it was out of the water. Mrs Angus could recall having seen Mr and Mrs Evans, the driver and the Permanent Way Inspector moving about in the front carriage but she could not recall having seen Simon Penny. As she left the train she anticipated the others who had been just a few feet behind her would have escaped as well.

56.　The train guard was *Mr W G Anderson* who was based at Swansea and had been a guard for 27 years. The train departed from Swansea at 5.40 and arrived at Llanelli, where it reversed its direction of travel, 12 minutes late. There were two passengers on the train from Swansea; both were seated in the rear coach. At Pantyffynon the train was delayed for a further 24 minutes awaiting the arrival of Mr Sharpe. At Ammanford Station a lady was waiting (Mrs Evans) and she asked that the train should wait until her husband came back from making a telephone call. When he came the train departed and Mr Anderson recorded the time as 6.48½.

57.　The next stop was at Llandybie where another lady (Mrs Angus) joined the train which then proceeded to Llandeilo. At Llandeilo a man (Mr Bailey) joined the train which departed at 7.07. North of the station a permanent way supervisor was at the trackside and he signalled the train over an area of flooded track using a handlamp. Having done so the supervisor joined the train and the journey continued at a reduced speed.

58.　Mr Anderson said the train slowed down to the 10 mile/h restriction to cross Glanrhyd level crossing and at that point he thought they were through the worst of the floods. At the time he was standing up in the van but moments later he was thrown off his feet, across the brake van and into the wall, striking his head and losing his glasses. As he was getting up and recovering his glasses, water poured into the brake van through a broken window and it was quickly up to his waist.

59.　The sliding door of the inner security cage had closed on impact and momentarily he thought he was trapped but he was able to reopen the door. Mr Sharpe came through and when he looked back Mr Anderson saw that although the brake van was in the river the rear part of the coach was still on the bridge and was dry. He and Mr Sharpe called for the passengers to come through to the back coach. He then heard the permanent way supervisor shouting out "mind the holes in the floor".

60.　It was then that he went into the front coach and found as well as the permanent way supervisor, Mr and Mrs Evans, Simon Penny and Driver Churchill. He made his way past the others telling them to catch hold of the luggage racks and spoke to the Driver. Mr Anderson told me there was no panic and he remembered that Simon Penny had pointed out that there was a frog in the water outside one of the coach windows.

61.　He told me that the permanent way supervisor got stuck in the gangway door and he went to him and helped by pushing him through and then followed him through the doorway but remained within the gangway connection at the front of the rear coach. He was attempting to help Mrs Evans through the doorway and through the water rushing in at the gangway connection when there was a cracking sound followed by an even louder crack and the front coach was swept away.

62.　*Mr A L Sharpe* was at the time of the accident the *Customer Services Manager* for British Railways' Area Manager at Swansea. He explained that while he was responsible for the passenger and parcel side of the business in the Swansea area he was also an operating manager and was regularly examined in operating rules and procedures. His previous appointment was as Traffic Manager at Woking on the Southern Region.

63.　During the weekend he had been the second 'on-call' manager. He was telephoned at home by Mr Scott at about 04.20 on the Monday morning. Mr Scott told him that there was flooding at Carmarthen and there also had been some flooding on the Central Wales line between Llandeilo and Llandovery. Following the telephone conversation Mr Sharpe went to Swansea Station where he arrived at about 05.05 hours. On arrival at the station he familiarised himself with the situation and the changes made to the train services following the flooding of Carmarthen. He believed the Shrewsbury train departed from Swansea approximately 5 minutes after he arrived and, because he understood the Permanent Way Supervisor was to meet the train at Llandeilo, he decided not to travel on it.

64.   At about 06.05 he was told by the signalman at Pantyffynon that the Permanent Way Supervisor had been at Llandovery but because the roads were flooded he had not been able to reach Llandeilo. Mr Sharpe told the signalman to hold the train at Pantyffynon and he would make his way there to join the train. He told me it was his intention to travel with the train to Llandeilo and then to reassess the situation there. He joined the train at about 06.40 and travelled to Llandeilo where it arrived at about 07.05.

65.   At Llandeilo Station there was a member of the Permanent Way Supervisor's staff, who told him that the supervisor was on the track some 100 to 200 yards north of the station where there was some flooding. He was also told that the Supervisor had authorized the train to travel as far as that place. Mr Sharpe said the train was driven cautiously from the station up to where the Supervisor signalled the train to stop with a red handlamp. Water was running between the sleepers of the track over a length of five or six sleepers.

66.   The Supervisor told them to wait and then Mr Sharpe saw him carrying a sleeper. Mr Sharpe got out of the train but by then the Supervisor had placed the sleeper under the sleepers in the track where some of the ballast had been washed away. He returned to the driving cab leaving the Supervisor by the right hand side of the track and relayed the instruction to the driver to proceed slowly over the flooded section of the line. This was done and the train was then stopped to allow the Supervisor to board it.

67.   The Supervisor joined the driver and Mr Sharpe in the driving cab and introduced himself as Mr J R Davies. He said to the driver that the other reports were of flooding around the 21 and 26 mile posts. Mr Sharpe said the journey recommenced and although he was not certain as to the speed of the train he thought it was about 15 mile/h. The driver made a brake application but the train did not stop because Mr Davies said "Oh, that's OK" so the driver released the brake. Mr Sharpe said that he could see some brown water between two sleepers in the track. He said Mr Davies then reminded the driver that the next location was at the 26 mile post.

68.   Mr Sharpe confirmed to me that there was a 10 mile/h speed restriction over the level crossing at Glanrhyd but he was not certain whether the driver had needed to apply the brakes to reduce speed for the crossing. He thought the train's speed was round about 10 mile/h and that the driver had applied more power because of the upward gradient to the bridge. Mr Sharpe said that he could see the abutment end of the bridge but as the train reached the summit of the incline he saw that the bridge had partially collapsed. The driver made an emergency brake application and said something like "Hang on".

69.   Mr Sharpe said he looked out of the cab side windows and realised there was no way out there but looking back he could see the rear coach was still on the abutment. He said he waded through the first coach to check if it was possible to escape through into the rear coach. He found the vestibule door between the two coaches was about half open. It was not easy but he was able to get through without too much trouble and he went back into the rear coach. He found that it was possible to step out of the rear passenger door on the right hand side of the coach onto the bridge girder.

70.   He told me that as he went through the first coach there was no panic and everyone appeared to be uninjured. Having established there was a way out from the rear coach he got back into the coach where he thought he saw two of the male passengers and called "This way out". He went to the connection between the two coaches and again called "This way out". Mrs Angus was coming through the doorway from the front coach and he thought his call was acknowledged by Mr Davies.

71.   Mr Sharpe said that he was concerned about the people still in the front coach and also about those who were by then outside the train. As there were other railway staff on the train he made his way out of the train and having checked with the three passengers outside the train that they were all right, made his way to the house adjacent to Glanrhyd level crossing to summon assistance.

72.   I asked Mr Sharpe particularly about the role he was fulfilling and the operating procedures adopted for the running of the train. He told me that with Mr Davies on the train he relied on his experience and judgement and, therefore, his own presence was not strictly necessary. He said that although he was the senior (in grade) member of staff present he was not actually aware of which regulations had been implemented because he had not been directly involved.

73.   *Mr J R Davies*, the *Permanent Way Section Supervisor* for the Llandrindod Wells Section told me he had been employed on the Central Wales Line for 37 years and that he had been the Section Supervisor for the last 5 years. From about 05.45 to 16.45 on that Sunday he had been supervising a gang doing trackwork to the north of Llandrindod Wells and had spent most of the day outside in the rain. At

about 22.00 he was telephoned at home by the signalman at Pantyffynon who told him that the driver of the 'light' locomotive returning from Craven Arms had reported flood water at three locations between Llandeilo and Llandovery.

74.   Mr Davies said he was not particularly surprised by this because the line had been flooded at 18½ mile post, which was very near to the river, on other occasions. At approximately 03.45 on the Monday morning he had a telephone conversation with Mr Scott who told him that he was going to travel on the Swansea to Shrewsbury train. He told Mr Scott that he would go to Llandeilo.

75.   He departed from his office at Llandrindod Wells by road being driven by a member of his staff at approximately 04.15. They had no difficulties until they reached Llandovery where there was a road closed sign on the A40 road. He telephoned the signalman at Pantyffynon from Llandovery Station to say that he could not get through by road but that he would try again later. Between 05.30 and 06.30 a number of vehicles were travelling along the A40 and the driver of one of them told them they would be able to get through. At 06.30 he again telephoned the signalman to tell him he was making his way to Llandeilo.

76.   The conditions on the road were better than Mr Davies had expected and there was water on the road at only three places all to the north of Llanwrda. From there to Llandeilo the road was clear and he reported to the signalman that he had arrived there. He was told by the signalman that Mr Sharpe and not Mr Scott was on the train.

77.   Before the train arrived he walked along the track to the 18½ mile post where he found the track clear of the water but some ballast had been washed away. He decided there would be no problem for the train to travel over it at reduced speed. The line at that point is on a sharp curve and the track is canted. He stopped the approaching train with a red hand lamp. For extra safety he placed a discarded wooden sleeper at the end of the concrete track sleepers. He then instructed the driver and Mr Sharpe that the train could go over at 5 mile/h.

78.   He joined the train and on the approach to the 21 mile post, which is on straight and level track he instructed the driver to reduce speed to between 3 and 5 mile/h. The train was able to continue over that section of track without any lurches or uneven riding. The speed of the train then increased to what Mr Davies estimated was between 10 and 12 mile/h. He said that the driver did not make a brake application for the 10 mile/h speed restriction at Glanrhyd crossing but allowed the train to slow itself down.

79.   The lights on the train were illuminating 20 to 25 yards of track ahead. His vision was concentrated in this area and as the train approached the bridge at about 15 mile/h he could see the ends of the bridge girders. As the train ran onto the bridge he noticed that just ahead it was distorted and simultaneously the driver applied the brakes. The leading coach went down into a dip and then started to fill with water. Mr Sharpe was the first out of the driving cab, Mr Davies said he was second and the driver followed him out. He made his way to the rear of the coach.

80.   He saw the guard there and two of the passengers (Mrs Angus and Mr Bailey) making their way into the rear coach. He had not seen the teenage boy but had seen Mr and Mrs Evans. He said he tried to encourage Mrs Evans to get out of the coach and assisted her to the end of the coach. Mr Davies struggled through the doorway to the rear coach with the intention of helping Mrs Evans through, but the coaches parted.

81.   Mr Davies was questioned by the legal representatives present at my Inquiry as to whether he should have interpreted an instruction in Civil Engineers Handbook No. 6 to mean that he should have examined the bridge on foot before the train ran onto it. He replied to the effect that that was not his understanding of the instruction which he believed referred to action he should take when carrying out routine inspections.

As to the Operating Procedures

82.   *Mr K Winder*, the *Area Manager* at Swansea was responsible for the operating but not the engineering of the railway network from the west of Bridgend to Milford Haven, Pembroke Dock and Fishguard. It included the Central Wales Line as far as Craven Arms. He had held the post for 2½ years and had previously been Area Operations Manager at Dartford, Kent. At Swansea he had 6 Operating Staff, two of whom were Mr Sharpe and Mr Scott, to assist him.

83.   He had been alerted to the problems caused by flooding by a telephone call at 04.00 from Mr Scott on the Monday morning and he arrived at his office at Swansea at about 05.45. He did not speak

9

to Mr Sharpe and was not consulted about his decision to travel on the train. He was, however aware of the intention of using the 05.27 from Swansea to examine the Central Wales Line following the reports of flooding. He told me that if Mr Scott had not suggested it he would have suggested it himself.

84.   I asked Mr Winder if other alternatives were considered and he replied that he did not consider there was an alternative. He did not believe it was appropriate to examine the line in advance of the first passenger train because with flooding the situation could have changed significantly between the time of the inspection and the time of the train. Also because of the long single line sections of the Central Wales Line to use another rail vehicle would have disrupted the train service. I asked Mr Winder if he had considered delaying the train until daylight and he replied that he had not because the reports of flooding were for specific locations and there was nothing to suggest at six o'clock that morning that the situation had deteriorated. It was his understanding that the train was going in to examine those known areas of flooding.

at odds?

85.   Mr Winder was aware of the flooding in West Wales from the television on Sunday evening but he had received no specific warnings. He had no arrangements in place to receive warnings of severe flooding and he would not have known the meaning of a "Red" flood warning.

86.   *Mr B J Norman*, the *Western Regional Signalling Officer* explained that the train signalling on any line is carried out by the signalmen on the basis of instructions known as "Block Regulations". These regulations vary slightly depending on the type of signalling equipment installed on the line. In all of these instructions there is contained a Regulation 9 which deals with the 'Examination of the line'. Such a regulation appears in the instructions for the Central Wales Line and is fundamentally the same as the regulations which are applicable on all other lines of British Railways. The relevant section of the instructions is at Appendix A.

87.   At my Inquiry Mr Norman read a statement prepared by the British Railways Board's Director of Operations on the purpose and use of Regulation 9. The statement is at Appendix B. If the examination was to take place in hours of darkness the driver must be accompanied by a competent person unless the train was fitted with a headlight. On the Central Wales Line all trains are fitted with a headlight. A passenger train would not be used if there was fog or snow falling. It would also not be permissible to allow a passenger train to enter a tunnel during the examination of the line unless the tunnel was not affected.

88.   I asked Mr Norman if British Railways had instructions about the working of trains through flood water. He said that the instructions were contained in the section of the 'General Appendix' headed "Traction Units - Movement when Permanent Way is Flooded". Normal movement of trains must cease when the water level reaches two inches below the top of the running rails and then 'Emergency running' at walking pace is permitted so long as the water is not more than 4 inches above the rails. This limitation was to protect electrical equipment rather than any risk that would be posed to the safety of the train.

Evidence as to the History and Maintenance of the Bridge

89.   *Mr B Bell*, the *Bridge Assistant* to the Area Civil Engineer at Swansea, said that an earlier superstructure of the bridge had been replaced in 1958. Records of repair work to remedy scours to one of the piers in 1929 had been discovered but the records did not identify the pier concerned. The bridge had been regularly examined in accordance with the laid down instructions and over the years the examinations had revealed the need for repairs to the underwater portions of the piers. Repairs were carried out in 1970, 1976 and 1982. He had personal knowledge of the work in 1982.

90.   During a routine inspection the bridge examiner found what appeared to be a hole on the upstream cutwater of pier 2. (See paragraph 10 for position of piers). Mr Bell arranged for a railway diver to examine the bridge and it was found that there was a fairly large undermining of the cutwater part of the pier and there were trees caught in the jagged hole. The part of the pier which carried the load of the bridge superstructure had not been damaged. A diving contractor was employed to carry out the necessary repair work.

91.   Mr Bell outlined the bridge examination arrangements which are set out in The Civil Engineering Department Handbook 6. Bridges were inspected in detail by a trained examiner once every six years. This involved as full an examination as was possible bearing in mind the physical conditions of the bridge. In the case of the Glanrhyd bridge, which was over water, a rail mounted inspection unit was used which enabled the examiner to get underneath the bridge steelwork. The examiner would also carry out a visual inspection of the underwater parts of the structure and, if there was any cause for concern, a diver would be employed to make a more detailed examination. A less detailed inspection would be made in each of the intervening years.

92.   The arrangements for bridge examination were modified in 1984. In the past, detailed examinations were carried out on a three year cycle rather than a six year cycle but the intermediate annual inspections were not undertaken. Mr Bell believed the present arrangements to be an improvement on the earlier system.

93.   *Mr T Humphries* was the *Diving Manager* for Diving International of Fishguard, the company who carried out the repair work to the bridge pier in 1982. He met Mr Bell on site and the work required was explained to him. The work was undertaken using a team of divers. First, a large amount of debris was removed from a scour in front of the pier. It included medium sized trees and parts of trees. A section of masonry about a metre square was found to have collapsed from the leading edge of the cutwater.

94.   Mr Humphries said the hole was cleaned out to a depth of about six feet below riverbed level and then it was coffer-dammed off by concrete bag work fastened together by steel dogs. Mass concrete was placed between the coffer-dam and the pier. This concrete was reinforced with steel rods. The concrete was taken up to above the water level. He said the repair work was not taken down to the foundations of the pier but merely to hard ground.

95.   While carrying out the repair work on the pier, road vehicles were driven through the shallow water and parked on the island formed of pebbles downstream of the bridge. One day during the work they were warned by a bailiff that there was a wall of water bringing rubbish and debris with it coming down the river towards them. They moved the vehicles from the river and almost immediately after they had done so the wall of water arrived at the bridge. There were trees and one particular large stump being turned over and over in front of the water which caused some damage to the uncompleted repair work.

96.   On 13 August 1987 he made an unofficial visit to the Glanrhyd bridge while returning with a diving team from inspecting a culvert at Cynghordy. The team of divers was a new one and he wanted to show them the repair that had been made to pier 2. They had not dived into the river but they had looked at all of the piers not just pier 2. Mr Humphries said there were no visible defects and the piers appeared to be in good condition.

97.   *Mr G Baron*, the *Assistant Area Civil Engineer* at Swansea was responsible for bridges, buildings and other structures in the Swansea area. He was assisted in his duties by Mr Bell. There were some 2,500 bridges and culverts in the area and some of the bridges were larger structures than the Glanrhyd bridge. Mr Baron said he was satisfied with the arrangements for inspection and the maintenance of the bridges. He had no reason to be unduly concerned about the safety of bridges in the Towy Valley.

98.   *Mr J N Thompson*, the *Area Civil Engineer* was responsible for all aspects of civil engineering in the Swansea area. His organisation consisted of a technical managerial work force, based in Swansea, with an out-based technical management to control Permanent Way works. It included beneath them a large number of track maintenance gangs who reported to six Section Supervisors. There were also two Works depots, one at Neath and one at Fishguard which carry out all work in connection with the maintenance and inspection of structures. His office organisation was split into three: his immediate assistant responsible for all the permanent way work, his Works Assistant, Mr Baron, and an Administration Assistant. Other managers and technical assistants were responsible to them for various aspects of the work.

99.   When the failure of Glanrhyd bridge and the seriousness of the river levels and the force of the flood came to his attention on the Monday morning he instructed that a check be made on other structures in the Towy valley between Llandeilo and Llandovery. Later that day one of the patrolmen carrying out the task had the misfortune to actually fall through the track and down behind the abutment of a cattle creep which had been washed away. The cattle creep was a small bridge of about eight foot span some 70 yds from the River Towy and 100 yds from the River Dulais and through which normally there was no water course. The effect of the flood had been to scour deep holes under the bridge and collapse both abutments inwards leaving the track and its ballast suspended above.

100.   At one or two other bridges undermining of the wing walls or scouring of flood arches was found at places where to Mr Thompson's knowledge similar problems had not been experienced before. His staff had also looked at the debris from the flood downstream of Glanrhyd bridge. Spread out over the fields where they had been left behind by the receding flood were a considerable number of trees. There were quite a number where the whole of the root structure, plus a considerable part of the trunk, had been carried by the flood waters. It seemed probable that some of these had been swept down river past the Glanrhyd bridge.

101.   I asked Mr Thompson about the views expressed by Mr Baron and Mr Bell on the condition of the bridges in the Swansea engineer's area. He said he found the general standard of the bridges to be

11

high and that a considerable amount of maintenance work had been done on them in the last 20 years. He did not accept the suggestions made that because repair work had been necessary to the Glanrhyd bridge at approximately 6 year intervals, it meant the condition of the bridge was deteriorating.

102.   I asked Mr Thompson about his interpretation of the requirement for Permanent Way staff to inspect bridges contained in Handbook 6. (The instructions are reproduced in Appendix C). Firstly, he said patrolmen, who walk along the line, and Track Chargemen in charge of a gang working in the area "shall observe the general condition of structures whilst they are working around it" and "If they see anything shall report it". Reports were received from permanent way staff who had noticed some minor defect.

103.   The instruction also requires the Permanent Way Supervisor to observe the condition of all structures during the course of his track inspections. The Supervisor is required once every three months to look underneath each underbridge and on top of each overbridge and also to confirm the effectiveness of each culvert and drain. It was Mr Thompson's personal view that although all of his supervisors did their best to comply with this requirement it was "quite an impossible task to expect of them".

Is it in the new HB6?

104.   Mr Thompson interpreted the requirement "During and following floods or heavy rain the Permanent Way Supervisor shall observe all culverts and bridges" to mean that whilst he was carrying out his regular inspections and if at that time there were floods, or had been floods or particularly heavy rain, he should take special note of any water courses. When asked what he would expect a member of his Permanent Way staff to find, when examining a line for flooding, he said he would expect them to look for water on or about the track which could affect the stability of the rails, sleepers or ballast. It was something which occurred many times a year in differing locations all around the Swansea area.

As to the site investigation and recovery of the wreckage.
105.   The work of accident investigation and recovery of the wreckage from the river was undertaken by British Railways' Western Region's Civil Engineer. The work on site was coordinated by *Mr A Pendleton* in close liaison with myself. Within 2 days of the accident, a team of engineers and surveyors had been assembled to carry out a survey of the collapsed structure.

106.   In presenting his evidence on the work that was undertaken, Mr Pendleton explained that it was clear from the outset that, whilst it was important to complete a detailed examination of the wreckage before anything was moved, it was limited in some respects by consideration for the safety of those undertaking the work. Of particular concern was the precarious position of spans 1 and 2 which were resting on the partially collapsed pier 1.

107.   The civil engineering contractors D.M.D were appointed to carry out the work. A 268 tonne capacity crane was erected on the Llangadog bank of the river and from that single position it was to lift the leading car of the DMU, all the bridge steelwork and sections of the collapsed masonry of piers 2 and 3 from the river. A preliminary investigation by D.M.D divers revealed the complex nature of the collapse. It was decided to use a Chartered Civil Engineering Diver to carry out underwater examinations. Shoreline Engineering Limited were employed for that aspect of the work.

108.   The sequence in which the work was undertaken is set out in Appendix D.

109.   The Shoreline Engineering Limited 4 man diving team was led by *Mr N J Bunch*, a Chartered Civil Engineer. The work was divided into two parts. Firstly, an inspection was made of the submerged steelwork of the superstructure. Subsequently, after the steelwork was removed an examination of the pier structures was made. All of the inspection work had to be undertaken in reduced visibility and fast flowing river conditions.

110.   Examination of the connecting trough unit between spans 1 and 2 revealed that all the connecting bolts between the trough unit No.1 and neighbouring deck section had sheared off on the Llangadog side. There was a displacement of 200 mm on the upstream side and 350 mm on the downstream side. A timber sleeper and other debris was jammed in the upstream half of the gap prohibiting examination of the cross girder beneath the deck section in this area. However, where access was possible on the downstream side, no evidence of major distortion was apparent. The four bolted connections of the cross girders on either side of the trough unit were examined and found to be intact with all the bolts present. No distortion or permanent movement of the joint was apparent, although cracking of the paintwork at the joint interface was apparent at all of the connections.

111.   Examination of the next trough unit connection revealed a similar situation to that at trough No. 1. The connecting bolts on the Swansea side were intact but those on the Llangadog side were all sheared. The displacement on the upstream side was 350 mm and on the downstream side 10 mm. The cross girder connections were intact but damage had occurred to the flange of the upper main girder at the downstream side halving joint and the connecting bolt was missing.

112.   Examination of the remaining trough units (Nos. 3 to 6) which were below water level was only possible on the downstream side because of the conditions on the upstream side of the bridge. All the bolts were found to be intact on both sides of the units with no apparent displacement having occurred between the units and the neighbouring deck sections. All cross girder connections were inspected and found to be intact with no movement or distortion apparent at the joint.

113.   Mr Bunch explained that deteriorating river conditions limited the extent of the pier structure inspection possible. The diving team was re-assembled on site on 29 November after the superstructure steelwork was removed and spent eight days inspecting the pier structures and retrieving sections of pier masonry for further examination.

114.   Pier No. 1 was demolished during the removal of the bridge superstructure. The masonry on the river bed prevented access to the base of the pier. The downstream anchor block complete with the bearing plate was retrieved but unsuccessful attempts were made to locate the upstream bearing plate, known to be separated from its anchor block.

115.   The masonry of pier No. 2 had been scattered on the river bed, and in order to log relative positions of the debris, a four pile grid was established around the perimeter of the debris. This then enabled the original pier centre-line to be established at river bed level. Hence, removal of debris and deposited material could be undertaken at the assumed foundation area. The displaced position of recognisable pier sections could also be related to their original position. Large pieces of the pier structure weighing up to 8 tonnes were lifted from the bed of the river. The main inspection work was undertaken by Mr Bunch.

116.   Generally, the original pier position was situated within a large scour hole. This was evident from the bed slopes rising upstream and towards pier No 1. Considerable break up of the pier and foundation had occurred. (The overall layout of the debris is depicted in Diagram No 4). The pier was found to have split into two parts, upstream and downstream. The upstream portion had its upper section sheared off at approximately 75 mm above the level of the remedial work of 1982.

117.   The remedial work consisted of a concrete bagwork shutter filled with mass concrete. The concrete bagwork had been stitched together and subsequently pinned to the mass concrete which had been brought up to the top of the bagwork and worked to produce a capping to the repair. There was evidence of river wear to both this concrete cap and on the exterior face of the bagwork. A number of the concrete bags had become detached from both sides of the pier leaving their impression in the mass concrete. Mr Bunch concluded that the bags had become detached only recently. The repaired section of the pier and some of the adjoining downstream masonry was lifted from the river.

118.   Considerable wear from river action was evident on the Llangadog side downstream masonry attached to the repaired upstream end. At around the lower extent of the bagwork shutter excessive wear on the neighbouring masonry blocks was apparent. Initially, this was considered to have been caused by accelerated river flow beneath the bagwork repair. However, further examination when the portion of the pier was retrieved from the river showed that this wear was, in fact, present at the time of the remedial work. There was very little evidence of river wear on the Swansea side of the pier.

119.   A second major area of debris was found at the downstream end of the centre-line of pier No 2. The downstream half of the pier had fallen towards Llangadog and parallel to the pier centre-line. Break up of the upstream end of this portion of pier had occurred as the pier collapsed onto its side. The river bed level in this area was rising and the pier section was lying with its downstream end approximately 1.20 m above its upstream end. It was not possible to gain access beneath this section and it was possible that other debris buried beneath it contributed to the break up of this section of the pier.

120.   At the base of the section of pier there was a wider stepped out course of masonry. There was no evidence of foundation or bed material attached to the underside of this course. A number of pieces of masonry in the order of 1.5 m square and 250 mm thick were found running along the centre line of the pier but on the Swansea side of it. Some of these slabs were recovered and attached to them was a material consisting of medium to fine river gravel cemented with lime mortar. Subsequent analysis by Thyssen GB Limited showed that this material was not naturally found around the base of the pier.

121.   It was assumed that these slabs had formed the pier foundations but it was not possible to decide which other pieces of masonry had sat directly on the foundation slab. There was no evidence of river wear on the pieces of foundation slab recovered. At a point midway down the centre-line, on the Llangadog side of the pier, a section of pier foundation which although broken and slightly rotated, appeared to be in situ. Considerable air lifting of deposited sand was carried out in this area and the complete slabs were exposed.

122.   Approximately a 900 mm width measured along the line of the bridge remained. Further material was air lifted from around these slabs to a level some 900 mm below the slabs. The natural bed material beneath the sheared off edge of the slab, on the pier centre-line, consisted of approximately 200 mm of fine to coarse gravel overlying a dark brown silty, fine to medium sand. This material appeared to be undisturbed. The edge of the slab on the Llangadog side showed extensive signs of wear from river action indicating that at some time the river bed level has been at or below the foundation slab level. Cemented river gravels could be felt on the underside of the slabs.

123.   Approximately 2.0 m upstream of its original position the upstream 'bullnose' foundation slab was found buried under recently deposited sand and gravels. It had rotated through approximately 90 degrees towards Llangadog. It was identified by its shape and the profile of the remaining mortar on its upper surface. Evidence of river action commencing about 0.5m from the upstream point was present and cemented river gravels could be felt on the underside of the slab. There was no evidence of any dowels or anchor pins between this slab and the remedial work carried out above it.

124.   In the area the 'bullnose' was found there were also random pieces of broken up mass concrete and some lumps of concrete overspill. In this area a number of the concrete bags used in the repair were also found. It was apparent that these bags had recently been dislodged from the repair. Moving downstream along the pier centre-line the river bed material below the foundation level was consistently found to be sand. At a point approximately 6 m down from the upstream end, and just to the Swansea side of the pier centre-line, a sample of the cemented river gravels was found overlaying a sandy silt. The cemented gravel appeared to be in situ but its upper portion had been dislodged and several large samples were found lying adjacent to but generally downstream of the original area.

125.   A large bank of material, consisting of both cemented river gravels and pier masonry, as well as recently deposited sand and gravels, was present at the downstream end of the pier. This bank of material prevented access to the downstream 1.5 m of the pier below the foundation level. Some of the downstream 'bullnose' sections of the pier were found lying in the vicinity of the broken up downstream half of the pier. The two bearing blocks, which supported the superstructure of the bridge, from the pier were found both lying downstream from their original position and to the Llangadog side of the pier. They were recovered with the bearing plates still attached.

126.   Approximately 60 per cent of the structure of Pier No 3 was present above water level during the course of Shoreline Engineering's second visit to the site. It was noted that the slight river flow alongside the pier was in the opposite direction to the general flow. River conditions prevented access during the company's initial visit when the bridge superstructure was lying in and diverting the flow of the river.

127.   The remaining portion of the pier was rotated slightly. The downstream portion of the pier was partially broken up and lying in pieces on the river bed. (This is depicted in Diagram 5). The method of construction used for pier No 3 foundation was clearly evident and exposed just below water level.

128.   This was a timber cofferdam incorporating timber walings and circular timber struts. It appeared that the cofferdam timbers had been driven approximately 1.25 m below the bottom of the final pier foundation. Excavation had then been undertaken to approximately 1.20 m below the top of the cofferdam. The base of the excavation was then levelled with a 300 to 400 mm layer of cemented river gravels. The pier was then built with a single course foundation slab and then conventional masonry construction above. The void between the cofferdam and the pier was then backfilled with cemented gravels and capped with mass concrete at a level corresponding to the top of the cofferdam timbers.

129.   At a point approximately 1.5 m from the upstream end of the pier, some of the vertical timbers of the cofferdam were missing. Through the gap a timber strut used in the cofferdam construction was visible passing under the pier and the cemented gravels. A void beneath the pier extended both upstream and downstream of the strut. Penetrations of a metre were possible beneath the pier and it appeared that the pier was being supported on the strut. Due to the irregular nature of the cemented gravels and the pier rotation that had occurred it was not possible to give accurately the general height of the pier undermining.

In the vicinity of the strut it was in excess of 150 mm and the base of the void was covered with decayed oak leaves.

130. It was possible to insert a probe into the void until what appeared to be another strut 750 mm downstream of the first strut was reached. The pier itself appeared to have rotated about the first strut with the downstream end lower. The exposed end of the horizontal waling of the cofferdam showed evidence that some of the missing vertical timbers had only recently been removed.

131. The downstream half of the pier had completely broken away and was standing in a scour hole at the rear of the pier. (The approximate river bed levels are depicted in Diagram 5). The displaced section of pier was approximately 1.00m downstream and lying at an angle. The rear of the pier had also rotated towards Swansea and dropped into the scour hole. Some loose pieces of masonry were found in the area surrounding the larger section of the pier. Some deposition of sands and gravels had subsequently occurred within the scour hole.

132. Approximately 1.5 m of the upstream timber cofferdam remained in situ on the Swansea side of the pier. The downstream half, on the Swansea side of the pier, and the end of the cofferdam was missing. No trace of these timbers was found downstream of the bridge although the timbers, with their metal driving shoes attached, have negative buoyancy. Generally, t.he tops of the remaining timbers indicated extensive wear from river action on the Swansea side. Some timbers showed wear along the vertical upstream edge caused by either lateral displacement into the river flow or exposure, as a result of the adjoining timber having been removed.

133. One of the vertical cofferdam timbers was removed from the midpoint of the Swansea side of the pier. There was no obvious indication on the timber of a recent lowering of the river bed level and the existing bed level was identifiable on the timber.

134. Mr Bunch told me that in his opinion the collapse of pier No 2 appeared to have been caused by mechanical action. The collapse of pier No 3 appeared to have been caused by the downstream end of the pier falling into a scour hole.

135. *Mr D B Dawson*, the *Works Design* and *Construction Engineer* in British Railways Western Regional Civil Engineer's office, summarized the results of the investigations in evidence to my Inquiry and also to the Inquest. He said that from the results of the investigations carried out during the removal of the wreckage he considered that the Swansea abutment, pier 1, pier 4 and the Llangadog abutment had all suffered mechanical damage due to the movement of the superstructure.

136. The steel superstructure was displaced from its alignment at piers Nos 2 and 3. The bridge was horizontally displaced 3.7 m downstream at pier No 2 and 4.4 m downstream at pier No 3. It was apparent that the bridge collapsed due to either sideways displacement of the steel superstructure off its supports, or the failure of one or both of piers No 2 or 3.

137. Mr Dawson told me that consideration was given to whether the flood water reached a height above the level of the underside of the bridge superstructure and thereby exerted a horizontal force on the superstructure. There were no accurate measurements of the flood level available but various site observations indicate that the level of the water in the river was probably about 0.5 m below the superstructure of the bridge. Thus it was concluded that the floodwater flow did not contribute directly to the sideways displacement of the bridge superstructure.

138. There was evidence of many trees having been swept down the river. Mr Dawson had considered the possibility that floating trees may have become jammed under the bridge's girders causing an uplift force on the superstructure reducing its effective weight and also transmitting to the superstructure a horizontal force, derived from the flow of the river, which would tend to displace the superstructure downstream.

139. If trees had jammed under the superstructure and caused its collapse, it would seem likely that some evidence of trees remaining trapped under the collapsed bridge would have remained. No such evidence was found. Calculations indicated that the likely uplift and horizontal forces applied to the superstructure from trees jammed under the bridge would be insufficient to displace the superstructure of the bridge. Mr Dawson had concluded that it was unlikely that trees had jammed under the superstructure and even if such a situation had occurred then the forces exerted would have been insufficient to have caused collapse by sideways displacement of the superstructure.

15

140. The diver's report indicated that pier No 2 overturned towards Llangadog. For this to have happened there must have been a force applied to the pier in the Llangadog direction. The horizontal forces, which may have acted on the pier as a result of the river flood conditions, were calculated using assumptions recommended by Hydraulics Research Limited. These calculations were very sensitive to the assumptions made and it was possible that the actual forces would be appreciably less than the calculated ones. Nevertheless, the calculations indicated that pier No 2 should not have overturned towards Llangadog under the action of river forces.

141. Since the forces derived from the river acting on the pier would have been insufficient to cause the overturning of the pier, it seemed likely that the cause was movement of the superstructure pulling the top of pier No 2 towards Llangadog. The position in which the two bearing blocks from the top of the pier were found on the river bed afterwards was appropriate to a movement of the bridge superstructure towards Llangadog and also downstream. This movement could only have been initiated by the collapse of pier No 3.

142. It is apparent that pier No 3 had material removed from its foundations allowing the downstream end of the pier to settle breaking the back of the pier. Then the downstream end of the pier migrated down into the adjacent zone of deeper scour. The upstream end of the pier also settled in the downstream direction. Such a failure of the pier would have caused the superstructure to move in a downstream direction. This movement of the superstructure caused secondary damage to the remaining part of pier No 3 which was tilted back towards Llangadog. The upstream end bearing block was forced off the top of the pier and dropped onto the flood plain on the Llangadog side of the pier. This secondary damage to the upstream end of the pier and the movement of the bearing block was consistent with the movement of the upstream main girders across the top of the skewed pier into the final collapsed position.

143. Mr Dawson outlined the probable sequence of collapse was as follows:

(1)   a scour failure of pier No 3 at its downstream end resulting in:

(2)   the collapse of the downstream main girders of spans No 3 and 4, which were supported on the downstream end of pier No 3, resulting in the general collapse of the bridge superstructure and

(3)   the collapse of pier No 2 overturned towards Llangadog by the moving superstructure. He considered that the events outlined above would have been virtually simultaneous.

As to the behaviour of the River
144. *Mr M G Todd*, the *Head Water Bailiff* on the River Towy for the Welsh Water Authority, had held the post since 1984 previously having been a Water Bailiff on the upper reaches of the river from 1977. He told me that the majority of his work was on the river bank.

145. He confirmed that over a period of time the river changed its shape with gravel shoals building up and then disappearing over periods of high flooding. He said that the large shoal of coarse gravel downstream of the bridge changed to varying degrees mainly after large floods. He knew that pier 3 was positioned on the Llangadog bank with a strip of land between it and the river. He said that the river changed its shape in this area but not to the same extent.

146. During the years he had known the river there had always been a gravel shoal extending from the Llangadog bank into the river upstream of the bridge. Sometimes it tended to come and go, probably due to scouring after a heavy flood, but had been reasonably stable. He had never, however, seen the bank right back to the pier. There were times prior to the large floods at the end of the seventies when the shoal had moved and the pier was standing in water.

147. He said that it was not unusual for the river to flood several times during each winter. He had been on duty during 18 October as the flood was developing. He had observed the river from the main road bridge at Llandeilo and he said that he had "never seen the river come up as fast as that". In the days after the collapse of the bridge he had seen the timber piles at pier 3 but said he had never seen them before.

148. I asked Mr Todd about the damage that could be caused by trees floating down the river. He told me that after a large flood, he had seen tree stumps or full trees which had fallen into the river as the bank eroded under the root system. If he or the other Bailiffs saw large trees in the river they would take action to have them removed. Following the flood in October many large trees which had been washed into the river were found throughout the Towy and Cothi catchment areas. There were far more than usual.

149.   I asked Mr Todd about the 'Fisheries releases' of water into the river from Llyn Brianne dam. He said that although the releases are phased to come out gently the water level does tend to rise quite quickly. The effect was of the water creeping up the gravel rather than a wall of water travelling down the river. He said that such releases did not cause much change to the shape of the river.

150.   *Miss J R Frost*, a *Hydrologist* with the Welsh Water Authority told me that during the weekend before the accident there was extensive flooding throughout the South West Wales area, as a result of between 50 and 200 millimetres of rainfall in a period of approximately, 27 hours. It commenced late on the Saturday evening and went right through until Sunday evening. The Welsh Water Authority received an initial rainfall warning from the Cardiff Weather Centre on the Saturday evening and the Duty Officer monitored the situation and opened the Flood Warning Centre on Sunday morning.

151.   The Welsh Water Authority use a series of stages of flood warnings which are issued to the Police. The preliminary warning is an "Amber alert". At this stage the Police may order other emergency services or local authorities to standby. This is followed by a "Red 1" warning of limited flooding of agricultural land or property. This in turn is followed by a "Red 2" warning of serious flooding with danger to life and property. The "Red 2" warning is the most serious warning that can be issued for the upper Towy. There is, however, a further "Red 3" warning which only applies to Carmarthen, and the lower Towy in the West Wales area. As with the Amber alert, the Red Warnings are also issued to the Police but they are public warnings and the Police liaise with radio and television companies.

152.   The details of the warnings issued during that weekend were:

Amber for the upper Towy	08.55 on Sunday 18 October
Red 1	12.23 on Sunday 18 October
Red 2	19.20 on Sunday 18 October
Warnings withdrawn	12.25 on Monday 19 October

Since 1980, when the system came into operation, it was the first time that a "Red 2" warning for the upper Towy had been issued. During the same period a total of nine "Red 1" warnings had been issued. The flood warning system was contained in an instruction booklet issued in October 1986. Listed within that booklet were the organisations to which it was issued; it did not include British Railways.

153.   The Welsh Water Authority maintain a gauging station at Manorafon 5.2 kilometres downstream of the bridge. Miss Frost interpreted the readings from the gauging station for me. The readings showed a peak level occurring between 22.00 on the Sunday evening and 01.00 on the Monday morning. The highest level was 3.81 metres, the highest level recorded since measurements began at that station in November 1967. With the river at that level the flow was spread over some 500 metres of the flood plain at the gauging station. The flow speed was calculated as a mean velocity of 1.71 metres per second but the maximum velocity close to the surface would be in the order of 1.5 times the mean velocity.

154.   By 07.00 on the Monday morning the level had fallen to 3.65 metres giving a mean velocity of 1.64 metres per second. I asked Miss Frost about the effect on the flow of the river being restricted to pass through the bridge. She said that the flow would probably be the same at the bridge, but as the flow is a product of area and velocity, so at the bridge where the area was constricted the velocity would be greater.

155.   I also asked Miss Frost about the effect of Llyn Brianne reservoir on the flows in the river. The reservoir is primarily for water supply and it was first filled during 1972. Prior to 1972, the flows coming down the river would have been completely natural. The effect of the reservoir in the catchment would be to slightly reduce the flood flows in the river. Even when the reservoir was full, the floodwater would spread out over the surface of the reservoir and thereby reduce the peak slightly. The reservoir had been full and with water over-spilling all the previous week.

156.   Water is normally released into the river through a discharge regulator at the bottom of the dam which remains open continually to maintain a compensation flow for fisheries and other requirements. During dry weather, in summer, if there is a need to increase the available water then the discharge regulators can be opened further. Such releases do not normally cause a surge down the river. Releases are also made for fishery purposes to encourage the movement of fish up the river. These releases do create a fairly rapid rise in the river but that is noticeable because the existing flow in the river is already very low.

157.   An examination of the Authority's records established the incident during the repair to pier 2 in 1982 when, according to the evidence of other witnesses, a "wall of water" travelled down the river as

having taken place on Friday 13 August. A rise of 1.18 metres was recorded at Manorafon between 09.30 and 11.30 on that morning. It appears this was due to the combined effect of a release of water for fishery purposes from Llynn Brianne and a very high river flow coming down the Sawdde, a tributary which joins the Towy immediately upstream of the bridge at Llangadog. This was an abnormal situation caused by heavy rainfall in a two hour period occurring an hour and a half after the release had commenced from Brianne.

158.   Hydraulics Research Limited carried out a study of the river's flow associated with the bridge. The work undertaken and the conclusions deduced from it were summarized in evidence to me by *Dr R Bettess*. He explained that three flow conditions were of interest. They were the nature of the flow immediately prior to the bridge failure; what the flow was like immediately after the bridge failure, when part of the bridge was in place in the river; and then the flow once the bridge and the wreckage had been removed. Of these it was only possible to investigate in detail the last case and the information obtained was used to draw conclusions about the flow conditions prior to the failure of the bridge.

159.   During December 1987 a series of hydrographic measurements were made. During the period immediately prior to the field observations rainfall had been low and the river levels throughout the assessment period remained low. The river discharge during the period varied from 33 to 102 m³/s.

160.   Ten individual cross-sections of the river were measured covering a stretch of the river approximately 350 m upstream and 150 m downstream of the bridge crossing point. A detailed survey was carried out of the river bed for a distance of 50 m on either side of the bridge crossing point. The data from these surveys was incorporated into a contour chart. The trajectories of the surface streamlines of the river were determined by using the technique of float tracking. The passage of each float was measured at several locations during its passage and the time of each observation noted.

161.   In addition to the above measurements, vertical profiles of stream velocities were measured using a current meter. Samples of the bed sediments were taken and a size analysis made. Use was also made of the British Railways' survey of the trash marks left by the receding flood water to provide an approximate indication of the highest water level achieved.

162.   The site survey work established that the main downstream flow of the river was to the right-hand side, that is, on the Swansea side of the position of pier 2. Towards the left-hand bank between the positions of pier 2 and 3 there was a large recirculating zone, or eddy with the flow travelling upstream. The surface velocities of these flows were up to 0.8 metres per second in the downstream flow and 0.3 metres per second in the upstream eddy.

163.   The size and occurrence of a recirculation zone was chiefly determined by the geometry of the flow, the geometry of the channel and the bend upstream of the bridge. It seemed likely that the recirculation zone was present with the bridge in place. An aerial photograph taken in September 1986 shows a sediment shoal in the area of the observed recirculation zone. This was consistent with an area of slow moving recirculating water which would encourage sediment deposition. This evidence, however, only indicates the presence of a recirculating zone at medium to low flows.

164.   In order to assess the flow conditions prior to the failure of the bridge it was assumed that the river bed levels at the bridge corresponded to those shown on a 1949 survey drawing held by British Railways. To estimate the velocities of flow in the channel it is important to assess the area of flow in the downstream direction at the bridge site. Two assumptions were considered: first that the flow was uniformly distributed over the total cross-sectional area of the river at the bridge, and secondly, the flow was confined to the right of pier 2. These assumptions give velocities of 2.36 and 4.7 metres per second respectively.

165.   Dr Bettess explained that in attempting to determine which of these assumptions was the most accurate consideration was given to the forces involved. Relationships were known which relate the velocity, the depth, the water surface slope and the roughness of the channel. Values for the depth and water surface slope were established from site survey work and using these the 'roughness length' associated with the velocities. The roughness length value for the 2.36 metres per second velocity was far in excess of what the river bed material would provide. The value for the second velocity of 4.7 metres per second corresponded closely to the bed material present. He said it, therefore, appeared likely that at the time of the collapse of the bridge the flow was confined to the right of pier 2 with an average velocity of flow of 4.7 metres per second, while to the left of pier 2 there would have been a re-circulation zone.

166.   It was difficult to estimate how large was the velocity in the upstream direction at the time of the flood. The highest recorded flow in the downstream direction was 0.35 metres per second while the

largest velocity recorded in the recirculation zone was 1.14 metres per second. If the same relationship existed with a downstream velocity of 4.7 metres per second then a velocity in the recirculating zone of 1.4 metres per second would have existed. For the purposes of calculating the scour a velocity of 1 metre per second was assumed.

167. In the calculations of sediment transport and scour it was assumed that the average depth, derived from the trash marks, between piers 1 and 2 was approximately 5 m while the depth of flow adjacent to pier 2 was taken as 6 m for the calculation of local scour around that pier. Established sediment transport theory was used to determine the amount of material in motion. Calculations indicated up to 1.6 tonnes per second of material was being transported at the time of maximum velocity. This was not a precise value but indicated that during the peak 3 hours some 17,000 tonnes of sediment could have been carried past the bridge. With this amount of material in motion significant changes in the bed of the river could have occurred.

168. The passage of a major flood past a structure in the river may have two general effects on the river bed. The flood may have an overall effect on the depth and the shape of the channel cross-section. For example there may be a general deepening of the channel during the flood. Secondly, the piers of a bridge alter the flow locally and may lead to scour in the neighbourhood of the pier. The amount of local scour depends upon the flow, the geometry of the pier and the nature of the sediment. In general terms the deeper and faster the flow the greater the scour expected, the narrower and more streamlined the pier the less the expected scour.

169. In calculating the scour at pier 2 consideration was needed of the effect of the repair to the upstream edge of the pier. Depending on which of the recognised equations for calculating scour depth was used and the width of the pier assumed, depths of 1.5 m to 8.4 m were calculated. Similar calculations for scour of pier 3 gave depths of 0.75 m to 2.2 m. In the case of pier 3 the scour would have occurred at the downstream end of the pier because of the reverse flow in the recirculation zone.

170. Calculations were also made of the horizontal forces imposed on the pier 2 by the flow of water around the pier. This force can be resolved into two components, one in the direction of flow ("drag") and one normal to the direction of flow ("lift"). With the pier exactly aligned with the flow of the water the lift force would be effectively zero. Observation suggested that the piers were not exactly aligned with the flow. As the direction of flow relative to the bridge pier at the time of the flood was not accurately known, an angle of attack of 10° was assumed. Values of 116 kN and 464 kN were derived for the drag and lift forces respectively.

As to Action taken following the Accident

In respect of bridgeworks
171. *Mr W Grant,* the *Regional Civil Engineer* made the following statement as to action and initiatives being implemented.

> "As a consequence of the failure of Glanrhyd bridge, the Civil Engineer's Department on the Western Region of British Railways has given urgent consideration to procedures relating to the examination of bridges, particularly those over active rivers, and to the means of ensuring the continued stability of such structures at times of above normal flows of water. All such considerations having as their ultimate objective the safe passage of all trains.
>
> The actions taken so far are, firstly, as you have heard from Mr Thompson, the police have been asked to pass Welsh Water Authority flood warnings to BR at Swindon, who in turn will pass them to the ACE's at both Swansea and Newport. These two Area Civil Engineers have issued their own local instructions on the action to be taken on receipt of the flood warnings of the varying severities.
>
> The wording of Paragraph 4.5 of Handbook 6, relating to Permanent Way Supervisors' inspections is being revised in conjunction with the Director of Civil Engineering at the Board.
>
> Consultation has started with Hydraulics Research on the criteria to be used to identify bridges most at risk in times of above normal flow.
>
> Instructions have been issued to the appropriate part of my office at Swindon to commence the preparation of a list of all bridges which at present receive underwater examinations. This list will form the basis of discussion to establish if any of the bridges are at risk.

[handwritten margin notes: "done?", "Yes.", "No issued though."]

Further actions have been identified for further investigation or action as appropriate. Firstly, other Water Authorities are to be contacted and suitable arrangements made for their flood warnings to be made available to the Civil Engineer's Department, so that all Western Region railway routes are suitably covered. Secondly, the frequency of underwater inspections is being reviewed, together with the method of carrying them out and the time of year that they are to be done. Thirdly, when the criteria for the identification of bridges at risk are finalised, as I referred to earlier, a programme will be established for determining the depth of the foundations of piers and abutments and action will be initiated should any shallow foundations be found. Within the criteria will be included the assessment of the structural strength of the bridge to resist hydraulic loading on piers and superstructure. Fourthly, in addition to the possible revision of examination frequencies and timings, I am considering whether additional records need to be kept: for example, the extended use of photographic techniques for noting changes of river bed levels after varying flow conditions and the use of soundings, or sonar, records to record the changing river bed configurations in periods of high flows. Fifthly, the staff responsible for the design of underwater repairs are to be given advice on their design to minimise the likelihood of scour or other adverse effects. Finally, the lessons learned by the Western Region will be passed on to other BR regions as soon as possible."

172. Subsequently, the British Railways Board's Director of Civil Engineering produced the following 13 point Action Plan:

"1) Hydraulics Research Ltd will suggest criteria to assist in identifying the rivers that are capable of behaving like the Towy in terms of scour and variability of flow rate.

2) The Regional Civil Engineers will consult River Authorities for advice as to which rivers meet the criteria. If the River Authorities are unable to help it will be necessary to resort to local knowledge and site inspections.

3) Regional and Area Civil Engineers will identify all bridges that cross the scour or flood prone rivers.

4) Regional and Area Civil Engineers will establish pier and abutment depths for these bridges.

5) If the Area Civil Engineers find any vulnerable bridges, they will produce a list that will be available to their on-call staff. The Director of Civil Engineering will provide guidelines to assist in identifying abutments and piers that are too shallow or marginal.

6) Area Civil Engineers will review records of the underwater inspections of all bridges over scour or flood prone rivers. Any bridges with deep foundations but which are in need of repair will be added to the 'vulnerable list'.

7) Area Civil Engineers will establish whether Flood Warnings are available for scour or flood prone rivers. If warnings are available, arrangements will be made for Regional Controls to receive them and promulgate them to Area Civil Engineers or the on-call officers.

8) Area Civil Engineers will, with the assistance of River Authorities, identify stretches of railway which could be vulnerable to flooding, through the presence of weak embankments or where underbridges, cattle creeps etc. could become watercourses under flood conditions.

9) Area Civil Engineers will devise instructions to cover the action to be taken in the event of a Flood Warning being received. The Area Civil Engineers must give specific guidance bridge by bridge to site staff detailing action to be taken as flood water rises, that is, at what point to impose a Temporary Speed Restriction or to close the line. The proposed system has to mean that if a supervisor cannot get to a 'vulnerable listed' bridge after, say, a Red Alert Warning, then the line must be closed, until inspection is in due course achieved.

10) Regional and Area Civil Engineers will review the present frequency of underwater inspections.

11) The changing shape of river courses will be monitored by photography or other means during 'superficial' examinations.

12) Regional Civil Engineers will ensure that all staff concerned with methods of repairing piers, cutwaters and abutments are made aware that:

a) The cross-sectional area of a watercourse should not be lessened by, for example, widening a pier.

b) The shape and surface characteristics of piers and cutwaters should not be changed in a way that worsens the character of the hydraulic flow past such structures.

This may mean that the practice of using bags of concrete as a permanent shutter or coffer dam is not appropriate.

13) When designing superstructure reconstructions over rivers, designers must ensure they know for certain the depths of abutments and piers. They should also ensure wherever possible that new superstructures are sited above any likely flood level, or are strong enough to resist water pressure or debris impact."

In respect of train operation

173. *Mr R J Poynter, the Regional Operations Manager* made the following statement:

"You are aware that the safety record of the railways has been built up over many years. A considerable number of the alterations to our rules and regulations have followed from lessons learned from accidents of varying degrees of severity. You are also aware of the well established system for reviewing rules and regulations that gives careful consideration to the need for changes and that alterations are regularly made to reflect changing circumstances.

I can confirm that the implications of the Glanrhyd accident are already under review by that process and that we shall carefully consider any recommendations you may wish to make on the matter."

174. Following incidents when bridges on the Western Region carrying the railway over a road were struck and damaged by road vehicles a Regional instruction on the action to be taken was published. Subsequently the following instruction was issued by the British Railways Board.

How is this promulgated by AR? General Appendix Item Section 6 + training & video.

"BRIDGES STRUCK BY ROAD VEHICLES

1. If it is reported that a rail over road bridge has or may have been struck by a road vehicle, movements must not be permitted over the bridge until it has been examined to ensure that it remains safe for the passage of trains.

2. The bridge may be examined by:

(a) an employee not below supervisory grade in the Operations, Civil Engineering, M & E E Engineering or S&T Engineering departments, OR

(b) any other employee passed as competent in these instructions by the Civil Engineer

3. Provided the damage is only superficial, the person concerned may authorise the resumption of the passage of trains at walking pace until the bridge can be examined by an employee in the Civil Engineering Department who is competent to examine bridges. When checking that the damage is only superficial, the person concerned must ensure that:-

(a) the vertical and horizontal alignment of the track appears normal

(b) there is no deformation or displacement or other damage (other than paint damage) to a metal bridge

(c) the displaced material on a masonry arch is nowhere more than 6 inches (150mm) in depth and the total area displaced does not exceed 1 square yard (1 square metre)

(d) the displaced material on a brick arch is nowhere more than one brick in depth and the total area displaced does not exceed 1 square yard (1 square metre)

(e) the internal reinforcing bars are not cut if exposed by damage to a concrete structure

4. The resumption of the passage of trains at normal speed must not be permitted until authorised by a Civil Engineering Department employee who is competent to examine bridges."

OTHER EVIDENCE

The bridge at Llantrisant

175. Shortly after I had heard evidence in public at Llandeilo I was contacted by *Mr G C Wyke*. He owned land adjacent to a railway bridge over the River Ely at Llantrisant. The land had a tendency to flood and in order to make it available for development he became associated in the late 1970s with a Welsh Water Authority River Ely Improvement scheme. Mr Wyke explained to me that as well as the

works adjacent to his own land included in the scheme was the placing of a concrete invert beneath the railway bridges. He told me that the Welsh Water Authority would not proceed without the work beneath the railway bridges. Mr Wyke, perhaps unwisely, agreed to pay for the works which he believed were the responsibility of the railway and the works were duly completed. He has subsequently without success attempted to recover the cost of the work beneath the bridges from the British Railways Board.

176.   He told me that he considered the Board was responsible for the cost because the works were essential to prevent serious scour undermining the bridge foundations. I understand from Mr Wyke that the Board's civil engineers involved at the time, while not disputing some scour was occurring, considered that the work undertaken was not necessary. Mr Wyke made available to me photographic and other evidence which, although not conclusive, indicates scour was indeed occurring and if it had gone unremedied could have affected the safety of the Paddington to Swansea line bridge.

177.   Mr Wyke's claims were re-examined by the British Railways Board's engineers. It is the BRB's opinion that the works were carried out beneath the railway bridges because the flood alleviation scheme created a need for a deeper channel beneath the bridges and not because of the existing condition of any of the bridges. On the balance of the evidence available to me I am inclined to accept that the BRB's engineers were in danger of not taking the problem of scour at Llantrisant sufficiently seriously.

THE INQUEST

178.   In accordance with the direction dated 7 March 1988 I acted as Assessor to HM Coroner for Carmarthenshire at the re-opened Inquest into the deaths of Sarah Patricia Evans, William Benjamin Evans, Simon Michael Penny and John Michael Churchill. The Inquest re-opened on 18 July 1988 in Llandeilo Magistrates Court and the jury returned their verdict on 20 July 1988.

179.   Following the public hearing of evidence for my Inquiry and prior to the re-opening of the Inquest the British Transport Police produced a file of papers which was submitted to the Dyfed Powis Branch Crown Prosecutor. After studying these papers, which included a transcript of my Inquiry, the Crown Prosecutor expressed the opinion that there was "insufficient evidence of the very high degree of negligence which would be sufficient to prosecute, with any reasonable prospect of success, either British Rail or a member of their staff for the manslaughter by neglect of the four persons who died."

180.   The Crown Prosecutor proposed that a final decision should not be made until after the Inquest was complete in case fresh evidence was to emerge, although, it was acknowledged that this was unlikely. In my opinion no fresh evidence of any significance did emerge.

181.   In his summing up to the jury HM Coroner drew attention to the opinion expressed by the Crown Prosecutor and said that

> "In other words, members of the jury, before you can bring in a verdict of unlawful killing, you have to be satisfied and satisfied beyond a reasonable doubt that any negligence that you may have discerned went far beyond ordinary negligence and constituted gross negligence, criminal negligence or culpable negligence."

And also

> "Indeed, the next matter you have to take into account is this, that a failure to appreciate that there was such a risk is not by itself sufficient to amount to recklessness."

I was in complete agreement with this statement.

182.   The jury, however, returned a verdict of "Unlawful Killing" on all four of the deceased. The case was then referred to the Director of Public Prosecutions.

DISCUSSION AND COMMENT

183.   Throughout the recovery of the wreckage and the site investigation I was closely involved in the way the work was being undertaken, the investigations necessary and the engineering conclusions being drawn from them. The conclusions drawn by Mr Dawson accord with my own interpretation of the evidence from the investigations. Damage to the various parts of the steel superstructure of the bridge, the geometry of the collapsed structure, the secondary damage to the abutments and piers, the positions in which bearing

blocks were found after the collapse and the scour marks on the bridge bearing plates were all consistent with the sequence of collapse triggered by the initial collapse of the downstream end of pier 3.

184.   The bridge was still capable of carrying load at about 21.20 on the previous evening when a 120 tonne locomotive passed over it. Indeed the locomotive stopped on the bridge and I believe that had Driver Rossiter seen any obvious damage to the bridge he would have promptly reported it. He would not, however, have been able to see any damage that by then may have been occurring to pier 3.

185.   The skew connections of the adjacent bridge spans and the stepped bearing arrangement of the main girders were rather unusual. I considered whether the connections between the adjacent span were sufficiently rigid to allow the bridge superstructure to remain suspended in approximately its normal position after the collapse of a pier. Calculations made for me by the Regional Civil Engineer's staff indicated there was not sufficient rigidity in the connections for the bridge to have been suspended in this way.

186.   Mr Carwyn Davies was the first person to see the damage to the bridge. He was certain that when he first saw it, shortly before the train came into sight, the bridge had already collapsed and was lying in the river. The evidence is, therefore, consistent with the train having run onto the bridge after it had already collapsed and was lying in the river. The evidence is, therefore, consistent with the train having run onto the bridge after it had already collapsed.

187.   As perhaps is to be expected the evidence of the witnesses as to the running of the train over the last part of its journey and the events immediately following its plunge into the river is not absolutely clear. With no firm evidence as to the time at which the various events took place I was unable to establish with any certainty the speed of the train after its departure from Llandeillo.

188.   I am satisfied that the speed of the train was properly reduced for the level crossing on the approach to the bridge. I believe that the evidence indicates that the train ran onto the bridge at or about 15 mile/h. Evidence from Mr Sharpe and Mr Davies suggests that there was no rapid acceleration nor would the short distance and rising gradient have permitted a large increase in speed to be achieved. During my Inquiry and again at the Inquest suggestions were made that the speed at which the train was driven was inappropriate for the conditions that prevailed. In my opinion these suggestions were unfounded.

189.   I believe that those directly involved in the running of the trains, that is, the driver and guard, Mr Sharpe and Mr Davies, did not appreciate the severity of the flooding of the river. They were concentrating on stretches of track where they had been warned there could be flood water on the track. The evidence given by Mrs Angus described conditions vastly worse than those described by Mr Sharpe and Mr Davies. In trying to make a judgement on this conflicting evidence I am inclined to accept that the men in the darkened driver's cab would have had a better view than Mrs Angus would have had through the windows of the illuminated passenger accommodation.

190.   I have given considerable thought to the appearance of the collapsed bridge. The inclined approach and the normal curved vertical profile would have meant that the centre of the bridge would not become visible until the train was at or close to the first span of the bridge. I believe the damage was not sufficiently visible on the approach to the bridge to enable the train to have been stopped safely short of the bridge. In the half light of that winter morning the first view those in the driving cab would have had was of the end of the main girders of Span 1. Despite the collapsed state of the other spans, it would not have been obvious from the end view of Span 1.

191.   After its initial plunge into the river the leading car of the train remained afloat for sometime. I have not been able to establish exactly how long this period of time was. All those on the train must have received a stunning shock as cold water swept into the leading car and the lights went out. The evidence from those who survived is generally consistent but as can be expected does differ in some details. I do not believe that any of these inconsistencies have any significance.

192.   Obviously initially there was confusion but it appears that moments before the leading car was swept away the evacuation was proceeding with commendable calm. With the guard positioned in the vestibule of the trailing car to help people through the corridor connection between the two cars, with Simon Penny following Mrs and Mr Evans, and with the driver bringing up the rear the situation must have appeared to be reasonably under control. The period of time that the leading car had already stayed afloat probably enhanced that belief.

193. Conditions at the gangway connection were never easy and clearly by the time Mrs Evans was attempting to pass through it the difficult conditions had become very much worse. This was presumably the beginning of the sudden final movement of the leading car and the tragic loss of those still in it.

194. During the course of my Inquiry and also during the Inquest it was suggested that either the use of a passenger train to examine the line under Regulation 9 was wrong or the regulation itself was seriously flawed. The first judgement that has to be made is whether those involved in applying Regulation 9 did so properly with the information available to them at that time. The second judgement that, I believe, has to be made is whether there are foreseeable circumstances where Regulation 9 is inappropriate.

195. In order that the railway may operate efficiently and avoid severe disruption to its services there is clearly a need for an operating instruction of the Regulation 9 type. I consider the use of Regulation 9 to overcome the numerous minor operating problems which occur to be both acceptably safe and in the best interests of the railway passengers. The need for such a regulation is clearly illustrated in the evidence given by Mr Norman and in the statement prepared by the Director of Operations. (Paragraphs 86 to 88).

196. The decisions to use the passenger train to examine the line under Regulation 9 was made in the knowledge that the line was flooded at three specific locations. On that basis the use of the passenger train was both appropriate and without undue risk. Although the proper form of words was not used by the signalman, I believe the conditions under which the train was entering the section of the line were correctly understood by the railway staff on the train. Indeed the approach to and passage over the first two areas where flooding was expected was with due caution.

197. The risk to which the train was exposed was, of course, not at the areas of flooding but the collapsed bridge at Glanrhyd and also the collapsed cattle creep bridge further on. The fact that these bridges had collapsed was not known at the time the railway staff involved made the decision to run the passenger train. I am sure had it been then different action would have been taken. Similarly, it was not known that either structure was suspect and the question of a railway structure being in doubt was not part of the decision making process in this accident.

198. In theory Regulation 9 could be used in circumstances when the condition of a bridge was suspect. I consider to do so would involve a higher risk than the usual application of the regulation. I believe this increased risk is unacceptable and the use of Regulation 9 if there is any doubt as to the integrity of railway structures is inappropriate.

199. During the course of my Inquiry it was suggested that rather than using a passenger train a locomotive should have been used to examine the line. This suggestion appears to have been made on the basis that while it is unacceptable to expose passengers to risk it is acceptable to expose railway staff to risk. I do not accept this; the operating procedures must be such that neither passengers or staff are put at risk. I believe if a locomotive had been used it is probable that it too would have plunged into the river.

Flood Warnings
200. It is clear from the evidence given at my Inquiry that British Railway Officers did not receive the flood warnings issued by the Welsh Water Authority. At that time, had they done so, they would not have understood or appreciated the implications of those warnings. I am pleased to report that this situation has now been corrected and proper arrangements exist in respect of warnings issued by the Welsh Water Authority. In the course of my Inquiry it has become evident that there is no consistent form of issuing flood warnings from the various Water Authorities.

The Engineering Aspects
201. There is always going to be a problem of knowing with any certainty the construction details of structures of the age of the majority of railway structures. Foundations present particular problems because they are hidden from sight. Even when contract drawings exist there is no guarantee that the structure was built according to the drawings; frequently unrecorded changes would be made to the design on site during the building of the structure. This is particularly true of the foundations.

202. Once the structure has stood for many years the adequacy of the foundations tends to be taken for granted. When subsequently changes are made to the structure, the foundations are regarded as satisfactory if the load upon them is not significantly increased. This was undoubtedly the basis on which the re-decking of the bridge at Glanrhyd was undertaken. Amongst the surviving design documentation there are calculations of the new loadings applied to the piers compared with the previous ones. (See Appendix E).

Calculations to determine brs at risk by mid '90 then prove foundation M'tce to be proved in 1990

suggest end '91

203.   It appears, however, that no attempt was made at the time to establish the depth, or form of construction, of the piers of the bridge or to make a proper engineering assessment of the adequacy of the foundations. I consider this situation to be unsatisfactory. The Director of Civil Engineering has recognised this and has implemented actions which should, in due course, establish the foundation construction of existing structures enabling proper assessments to be made and appropriate action to be taken to strengthen foundations whose stability may be doubtful.

204.   The difficulties of inspecting and establishing the construction of underwater foundations are considerable and should not be underestimated. The development of means of establishing foundation details without having to excavate to expose the foundations will considerably ease this task.

205.   I regret to report that in my opinion many of the British Railway's engineers involved in the maintenance of structures in or over watercourses did not have sufficient understanding of the complex behaviour of rivers, such as the Towy, when in flood. Many of those involved were, of course, exceptionally capable and experienced engineers but were not specialists in the narrow specialism involved. The use by British Railways of Hydraulics Research Ltd to provide the appropriate expertise is a responsible and appropriate response.

206.   I believe the limited knowledge is illustrated by two of the actions taken by British Railways prior to the failure of the bridge at Glanrhyd. Firstly, the repair carried out to Pier No. 2 of the Glanrhyd Bridge in 1982, while ensuring the structural strength of the masonry of the pier, actually increased the likely damage to the pier from scour of the foundation. Secondly, whether it was necessary to the need to carry out remedial work to limit the scour occurring beneath the bridge at Llantrisant. Mr Wyke's claims are disputed by the British Railways Board and there is no conclusive evidence as to what the situation was before the flood alleviation works were undertaken. Nevertheless, there is evidence that even prior to the scheme being implemented the river bed was already being significantly eroded.

The Inquest

207.   Deaths, which occur during the working of a railway, are one of the situations which require the Inquest to be heard before a jury. In such cases the verdict returned is a matter entirely for the jury. It was the judgement of the jury in this case that the appropriate verdict was "Unlawful Killing".

208.   This verdict had two effects on my Inquiry. Firstly, it meant it was inappropriate to publish my report before any decision was reached by the Director of Public Prosecutions. Secondly, and perhaps more seriously, I considered it inappropriate to discuss some aspects of the case with Officers of the Railway while it was possible that any agreements reached with them could be interpreted as evidence of previous fault which may have then been used in any prosecution. This led to a delay in finalizing some of the changes recommended in this report.

209.   The Director of Public Prosecutions announced in September 1989 that no prosecutions were to be brought in respect of the accident.

CONCLUSIONS

210.   I conclude that the bridge collapsed at sometime between 21.15 on Sunday 18 October and 07.00 on Monday 19 October 1987 during an abnormally severe flood of the River Towy. The collapse was caused by the failure of one of the bridge piers which was undermined by the scouring action of the river.

211.   During the course of my Inquiry two allegations received widespread publicity. I consider that both were without any justification whatsoever. The first was that the Welsh Water Authority deliberately discharged a large volume of water from Llyn Brianne reservoir and so made the flooding worse. The evidence from Miss Frost (paragraphs 150 to 157) shows that this was not so and the Welsh Water Authority issued a statement to this effect.

212.   The second was that the passenger train was deliberately used to test a suspect bridge. This claim I again consider to be completely without substance. None of the railway staff involved in the decision to use the passenger train to 'Examine the line' either knew of or anticipated that there would be any serious damage to any bridge which would have put the safety of the train at risk. The first person to become aware that the bridge had collapsed was Mr Carwyn Davies and that was only moments before the train ran onto the bridge.

213. I am satisfied that prior to the collapse there were no visual indications to those who were responsible for examining the bridge that its stability was in any way in danger. Nevertheless, I consider that there existed and had existed for many years a lack of understanding within many levels of railway engineers of the complex hydraulic behaviour of watercourses. In particular the rapid changes that can occur in river bed levels was not appreciated. I consider the past arrangements whereby bridge superstructures were replaced without any check being made on the existing foundation construction to be unwise.

RECOMMENDATIONS

214. Although I believe there to have been no intention in the events that preceded the Glanrhyd accident to allow the train onto a section of railway where the integrity of any part of the structure was suspect, the wording of the various forms of Block Regulation 9 did not actually make this clear. It is implicit from other Rules and Regulations that Regulation 9 must be used only when the signalman is reasonably able to assume that any structure is intact and safe. Nevertheless I consider that this important condition should be explicitly contained within Regulation 9 and I recommend that an appropriately worded preamble should be inserted in the Regulation. I understand that this recommendation would be acceptable to the British Railways Board.

215. The conditions imposed on the depth of flood water through which trains may be operated is based on the need to avoid damage to and the possible stranding of the train and not the risk of damage to the track formation. I recommend that the regulations should be strengthened to prohibit the operation of trains normally or under Regulation 9, regardless of the depth of water, if the floodwater is believed to be flowing and there is a risk of ballast being washed or disturbed. I again understand that this would be acceptable to the British Railways Board.

216. The conditions and form of inspection to be employed when there is doubt as to the integrity of railway structures needs to be clearly laid down. The General Appendix instruction regarding the action to be taken following the striking of a bridge by a road vehicle lays down the action to be taken in that specific case. I believe that the British Railways Board should consider producing similar instructions for occasions when railway structure may have been damaged in other ways.

217. The incidence of railway bridges being damaged by flood waters are, fortunately, relatively rare. Nevertheless on 7 February 1989 the viaduct at Inverness carrying the railway over the River Ness was destroyed during a severe flood. The risk to the bridge was perceived in advance of its collapse and the line had been closed to traffic. Also in Scotland a man fishing adjacent to Girvan viaduct on 11 September 1989, noticed that the foundations had been damaged. The bridge was immediately closed for repairs to be carried out.

I didn't think so

218. These further incidents together with the failure of the Glanrhyd bridge emphasize the importance of the Action Plan produced by the Director of Civil Engineering to identify these bridges which are susceptible to damage by river action. The British Railways Board issued Civil Engineering Department Handbook No. 47 - "Assessment of the Risk of Scour". This document prepared by Hydraulic Research Ltd was issued in May 1989. I understand the consultations with the Water Authorities are well in hand. I recommend that the consequent action required by the Action Plan should be implemented as quickly as possible.

which as the of AR

how long? depends on what H/book 47 throws up!

219. Finally, I wish to express my admiration for the calmness and courage of the passengers who found themselves in the most frightening of situations following the train's plunge into the river and, in particular, to Simon Penny who appears to have behaved in a most commendable way. I would also like to commend the actions of Mr Churchill, the driver of the train, who was clearly bringing up the rear and trying to ensure that all the passengers made their way out of the train, and to Mr Anderson, the guard of the train, who though immediately after the accident was in a place of relative safety entered the flooded coach in an attempt to confirm that those still in it were making their way to the rear coach.

A COOKSEY

Deputy Chief Inspecting
Officer of Railways

Some difficulties with H/book 47
Very sensitive to ground type under foundations
Rock gives zero foundation depth
Sand/gravel needs 30 metres!

LIST OF APPENDICES

A. Extract from Regulations for Train Signalling – Regulation 9.

B. Statement by the Director of Operations, BRB.

C. Extract from Civil Engineering Handbook No. 6.

D. Sequence of Recovery Work.

E. Glanrhyd Bridge - Pier Loadings.

LIST OF DIAGRAMS

1. Line Map.

2. Layout of Diesel-Multiple Unit Car.

3. General Arrangement of the Bridge.

4. Sketch of Collapsed Pier 2.

5. Sketch of Collapsed Pier 3.

EXTRACT FROM REGULATIONS FOR TRAIN SIGNALLING BY THE 'NO SIGNALMAN' TOKEN SYSTEM ON SINGLE LINES WITH REMOTE CROSSING LOOPS (NSTR)

9. **Examination of Line**

9.1 *Conditions and Method of Signalling*

When it is required in accordance with Regulations 4 and 5 to ascertain whether a line is clear, a train other than a Class 9 may be allowed to enter the section for this purpose subject to the following conditions:-

(i) the train must be dealt with in accordance with Regulation 3, the Driver informed of the circumstances and instructed to proceed cautiously, prepared to stop short of any obstruction;

(ii) during fog or falling snow a train conveying passengers must not be used;

(iii) if there is a tunnel in the affected section, a train conveying passengers must not be allowed to enter the tunnel unless the tunnel is not affected or it has been established that the tunnel is clear, if necessary by a member of the train crew walking through;

(iv) the Driver must be accompanied by a competent person in the following circumstances:-

– during fog or falling snow;

– during darkness unless a headlight (fixed or portable) is available;

– in a tunnel unless it is illuminated or a headlight (fixed or portable) is available.

STATEMENT BY THE DIRECTOR OF OPERATIONS BRITISH RAILWAYS BOARD.

Examination of the Line

1. The Regulations for Train Signalling permit a train to enter a section to ascertain whether the line is clear and safe for the passage of trains.

2. The circumstances in which this arrangement is most commonly used are:

(a) a suspected track defect following a report of a bump or lurch by the Driver of the previous train

(b) a track circuit showing occupied when the line is thought to be clear

(c) a suspected obstruction of the line following a report from a Driver or other person

(d) after the passage of a train from which a passenger may have fallen or some part of a vehicle or its load may have become detached

3. The Signalman is responsible for arranging the examination in accordance with Block Regulation 9. The essential requirements are:-

(a) the previous train has passed clear

(b) the train used for examination must be able to stop quickly and short of any obstruction; accordingly, a train on which the continuous brake is not in operation must not be used for this purpose

(c) because of the additional risks involved, a passenger train must not be used during fog or falling snow; similarly, it must not enter a tunnel unless it is certain that the tunnel is clear

(d) the Driver must be accompanied during fog or falling snow and, unless the train is fitted with a headlight, during darkness or when passing through a tunnel

(e) the Signalman must give the Driver the necessary information and instructions

The above requirements are slightly less restrictive when examining the line in connection with a track circuit failure.

4. Block Regulation 9 is probably the most commonly used of the emergency signalling regulations (especially on track circuited lines). The onus for instituting the arrangements rests with the Signalman. He must also give the necessary directions to the Driver who is required to report, after examining the line, whether it is clear. Where it is necessary for the Driver to be accompanied, this person must be competent for the purpose. Generally this amounts to being no more than a fit and able person, competent to assist the Driver in spotting the suspected obstruction (fallen tree, body on the line, etc). If, however, the line is being examined in connection with a track defect, normal working must not be resumed until a competent member of the Engineering Department has given such permission. He may examine the line with the driver of the examining train or he may do so independently.

5. The collapse of a viaduct, bridge, embankment or tunnel without any previous warning of a problem is a very rare occurrence indeed, such is the traditional standard of railway civil engineering. If, however, warning of such a possibility is given, the normal practice is for the line to be closed until the structure (etc) concerned is examined by a competent engineer. This procedure is applied when, as sometimes happens, a large road vehicle collides heavily with a railway bridge.

[handwritten: But not always?]

In the absence of any warning of such a possibility, the procedure for examining the line presumes that the line is fit to run on or, if that is not the case, it will become apparent to the driver. At the very worst, what might reasonably be expected is a minor bump or derailment at slow speed. This procedure has been invoked without incident on many thousands of occasions in many diverse circumstances.

(*Signed*) M C HOLMES

Director of Operations

13 November 1987

EXTRACT FROM CIVIL ENGINEERING DEPARTMENT HANDBOOK NO. 6

"EXAMINATION OF STRUCTURES"
4. Responsibilities of Permanent Way Staff

4.1 During routine examination of the track the Patrolman or Track Chargeman shall observe the general condition of all structures in so far as they may be visible from the track, and shall report to the Permanent Way Supervisor any obvious new defect or development of old defects.

4.2 The Permanent Way Supervisor shall observe the condition of all structures (including tunnels) in his Section, whether maintained by the British Railways Board or not, preferably under traffic, during the course of his track inspections. He shall note especially the development of new cracks or worsening of old cracks, fallen or displaced bricks or masonry, displacement of girders on bearings, signs of any impact by vehicles, walls out of plumb, loss of ballast, etc.

4.3 The Permanent Way Supervisor shall arrange for floor plates, pockets in girder work, and refuges in parapets of underbridges to be cleared of rubbish at least once a month. He shall ensure that the use of bars, picks or other sharply pointed tools does not damage any waterproof coating which may exist. He shall also arrange for embankment and cutting slopes to be cleared of undergrowth to permit efficient examination and ensure adequate drainage away from the structure.

4.4 Once every three months the Permanent Way Supervisor shall look underneath each underbridge and on top of each overbridge, and confirm the continuing effectiveness of each culvert and drain. Underbridges which are known to be frequently struck by road vehicles shall be observed from road level at intervals of less than three months, to be determined by the Area Civil Engineer.

4.5 During and following floods of heavy rain the Permanent Way Supervisor shall observe all culverts and bridges over water courses so that any washing away of the beds or banks of the water courses or any obstructions to the waterways can be quickly discovered. After storms or high seas he shall be on the lookout for any damage to sea defence works which could put the railway at risk.

4.6 The Permanent Way Supervisor shall periodically observe the condition of all large advertisement boards on or adjacent to the Board's property.

4.7 In the event that the Permanent Way Supervisor sees or is advised of anything abnormal, he shall inform the appropriate Works Supervisor.

4.8 Where, in the opinion of any member of the permanent way staff, the condition of a structure calls for urgent action, e.g. undermining of the foot of an abutment or wall, he shall send an urgent message from the site to the Area Civil Engineer or a senior member of his Works staff. If there is doubt about the safety of any structure immediate precautions must be taken to protect traffic.

4.9 Any unauthorised use of spaces under bridges or arches must be reported to the Area Civil Engineer.

4.10 The Area Civil Engineer must be informed if there is any evidence to show that vehicles crossing overbridges exceed the weight restriction indicated on warning notices.

4.11 In Tunnels any obvious movement in the lining, excessive scaling or looseness in the rock face must be reported immediately to the Area Civil Engineer, and if there is any doubt about safety, precautions must be taken to protect traffic. Any local instructions in connection with the examination of the tops of air shafts and of the land above the tunnels must also be observed.

4.12 In respect of certain side-of-line bridges, viaducts and bridges where it would be unreasonable for the Permanent Way Supervisor to observe the condition of every span, the Area Civil Engineer shall make alternative arrangements and inform the permanent way staff accordingly.

4.13 The Permanent Way Supervisor shall advise the appropriate Works Supervisor of the dates and times when permanent way work involving the removal of longitudinal timbers, ballast etc. will be carried out on bridges so that a detailed examination can be made of the parts thus exposed.

SEQUENCE OF RECOVERY WORK

16th November 1987:

The leading coach was carefully lifted from the river and set aside for inspection. The steelwork was inspected for signs of accident damage below and above water level. The extent of this work was limited by safety and visibility.

17th November 1987:

The cross girder connections at each end of span 4 were flame cut and the unit was lifted out in one piece. This part of the bridge was removed first as a trial for the more difficult sections to come. Furthermore it created a relief channel should the Towy flood once more.

18th November 1987:

Shoreline Engineering carried out an initial survey of pier 2 between the lift attempts made on span 4.

19th November 1987:

Overnight rain raised river level approximately 6 feet preventing any further diving. Debris on the River Towy was floating at approximately 6 m.p.h. Span 5 was lifted out for scrap.

20th-24th November 1987:

Spans 1 and 2 were cleared of debris and the Swansea end of span 1 was jacked up to clear the abutment. Pier 1 was then demolished by explosives, bringing spans 1 and 2 to the ground. At this time, it was also confirmed that the bridge paint contained lead, requiring full HASWA measures to be taken. After burning, half of span 1 was lifted out of the compound for scrap.

25th November 1987:

Test piling was carried out to establish rock level beneath the river adjacent to pier 3. Also, the underwater cutting of span 3 commenced using a thermic lance.

26th November 1987:

Test piling was carried out to establish rock level beneath the river between piers 1 and 2. Part of the deck and the downstream beam of span 1 were lifted out, followed by the span 1/2 deck section, and finally the upstream girder of span 1. The underwater burning of span 3 continued.

27th November 1987:

The underwater burning of span 3 continued, but was difficult due to the poor visibility caused by thermic lance.

28th November 1987:

Span 3 was finally halved and lowered to bed level. It was then reslung, lifting out the Llangadog half first, followed by the remainder of span 3 and part of span 2 in one lift.

29th November 1987:

The remainder of span 2 was lifted out of the river.

30th November 1987:

The Shoreline divers established the outline of the pier 2 debris and 4 No. tubular steel piles were driven to form the basis of a reference grid. The grid was then surveyed by the survey team and set out at the back of the site compound.

The idea of the reference piles was to enable the divers to lay chainage ropes and thus fix the position of the collapsed pier. Any significant finds would then be lifted out and put into position on the land based grid for further inspection. This system was also an excellent aid to the divers who had difficulty keeping their bearings, due to current reversals and visibility which sometimes went down to 1-2 feet.

1st December 1987:

The intact lower portion of the upstream pier nose and concrete bagwork repair were recovered and positioned on the land based grid. In an attempt to establish foundation level, worn masonry from behind the upstream nose of pier 2 was recovered.

31

2nd December 1987:

Further attempts to tie the worn masonry to foundation level proved fruitless. Hence the relationship between the bagwork repair and foundation level could not be proven, and so a change of approach was needed. Furthermore, 30 m.p.h. winds hampered the use of the crane.

The pier 2 centreline was set out on the river bed to assist in the classification of the masonry strewn over the area. This drew attention to the sheared side of a slab which looked as if it could be in its original position.

3rd December 1987:

Some 20 tonnes of debris were slung by hand and lifted off the centreline of pier 2. They were placed in a temporary position as winds hampered crane working.

Pier 3 was given a preliminary inspection revealing the probable method of construction and shallow foundation level.

4th December 1987:

Shoreline Engineering used an 'Air lift' to clear sands and gravels. The upstream bearing block of pier 1 was recovered and the clearance of pier 2 commenced. The pier 1 upstream and pier 3 downstream bearing blocks were recovered and the upper central section of pier 3 was lifted clear to allow better access.

To the Swansea side of the pier 2 centreline, a piece of manmade in situ concrete gravel was discovered, founded on sandy silt.

5th December 1987:

Further air lifting along the pier 2 centreline confirmed the existence of a 1000mm. × 900mm. foundation slab lying in its original position.

A number of samples were taken from both the river bed and from the recovered materials which have since been analysed by Thyssen (G.B.) Ltd.

Pier 3 was also air lifted for further examination.

6th December 1987:

The air lifting of pier 3 was completed and samples were taken for analysis by Thyssen (G.B.) Ltd.

After a further look at pier 2, the pier foundation nose, located in the upstream scour holes was air lifted for further examination.

7th December 1987:

Bed levels were taken around pier 3 and across the river.

A worn 12" × 4" timber coffer dam pile was removed to try and establish whether the drop in bed level was recent.

A trial hole was excavated to the Swansea side of pier 4.

Printed in the United Kingdom for HMSO
Dd 291893 4/90 C7 98637 0488/4 O/N 101996 9643

GLANRHYD BRIDGE — PIER LOADINGS

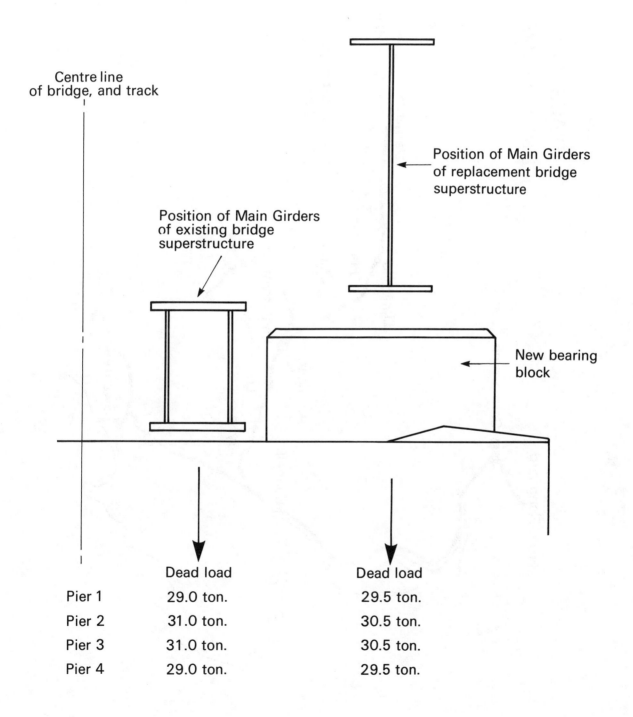

Centre line
of bridge, and track

Position of Main Girders
of existing bridge
superstructure

Position of Main Girders
of replacement bridge
superstructure

New bearing
block

	Dead load	Dead load
Pier 1	29.0 ton.	29.5 ton.
Pier 2	31.0 ton.	30.5 ton.
Pier 3	31.0 ton.	30.5 ton.
Pier 4	29.0 ton.	29.5 ton.

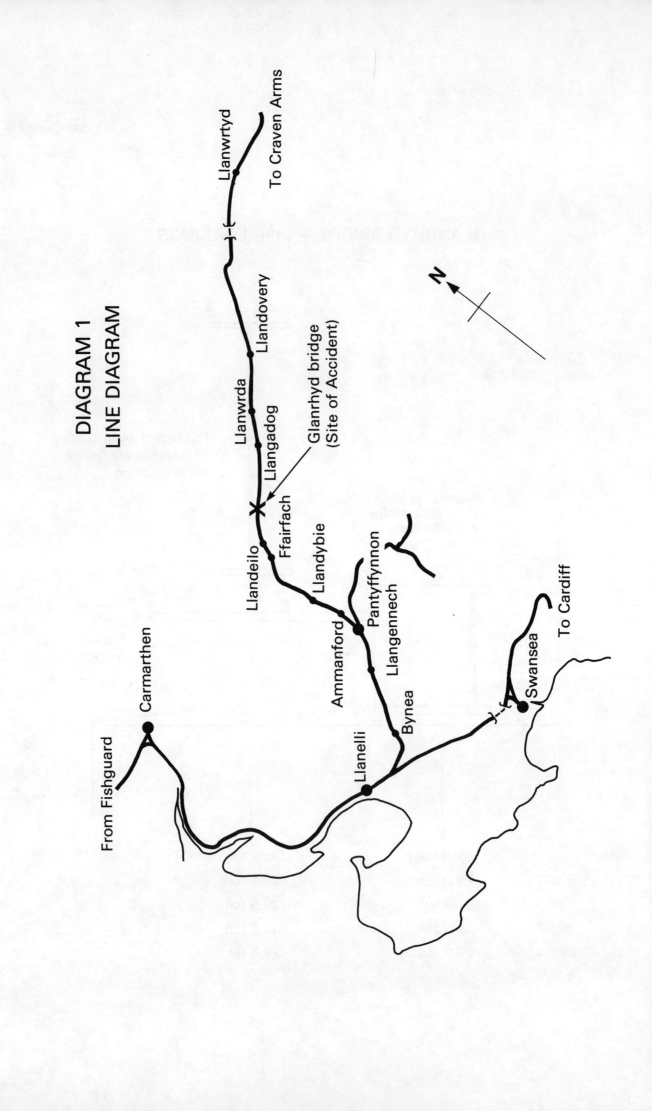

DIAGRAM 1
LINE DIAGRAM

From Fishguard

Carmarthen

Llandeilo

Llanwrda

Llangadog

Glanrhyd bridge
(Site of Accident)

Llandovery

Llanwrtyd

To Craven Arms

Ffairfach

Llandybie

Ammanford

Pantyffynnon

Llangennech

Bynea

Llanelli

Swansea

To Cardiff

N

DIAGRAM 2

LAYOUT OF LEADING CAR OF DIESEL-MULTIPLE-UNIT TRAIN

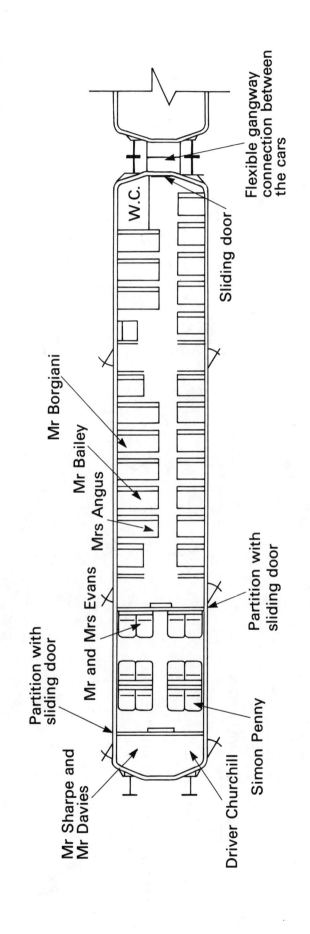

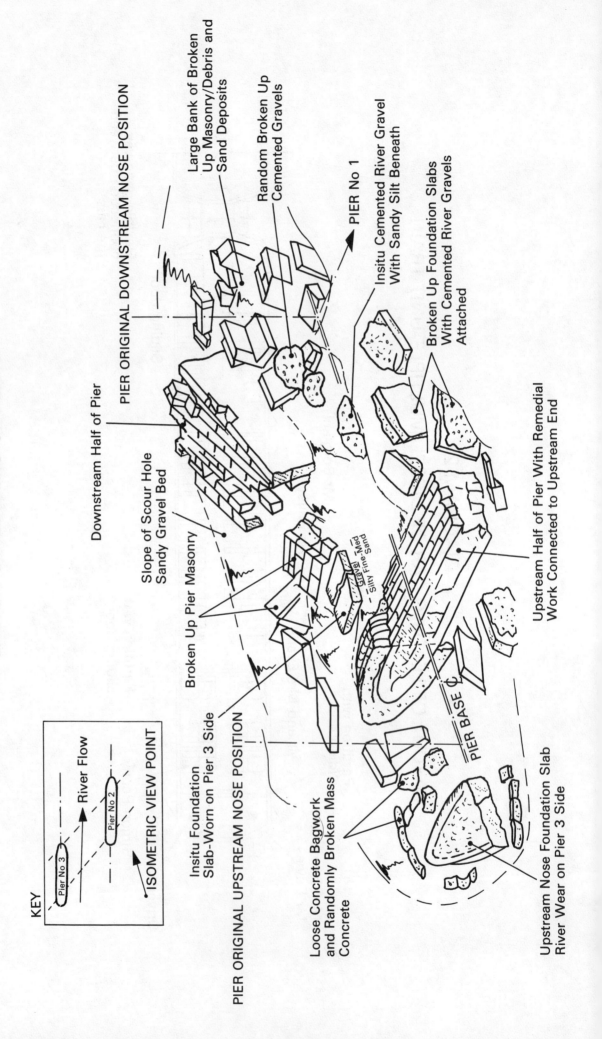

DIAGRAM 4

SKETCH OF REMAINS OF PIER 2

KEY

River Flow

Pier No 3

Pier No 2

ISOMETRIC VIEW POINT

PIER ORIGINAL UPSTREAM NOSE POSITION

PIER ORIGINAL DOWNSTREAM NOSE POSITION

Large Bank of Broken Up Masonry/Debris and Sand Deposits

Random Broken Up Cemented Gravels

PIER No 1

Insitu Cemented River Gravel With Sandy Silt Beneath

Broken Up Foundation Slabs With Cemented River Gravels Attached

Downstream Half of Pier

Slope of Scour Hole Sandy Gravel Bed

Broken Up Pier Masonry

Gravel Med Silty Fine Sand

Upstream Half of Pier With Remedial Work Connected to Upstream End

PIER BASE ₵

Insitu Foundation Slab-Worn on Pier 3 Side

Loose Concrete Bagwork and Randomly Broken Mass Concrete

Upstream Nose Foundation Slab River Wear on Pier 3 Side

DIAGRAM 5

SKETCH OF REMAINS OF PIER 3

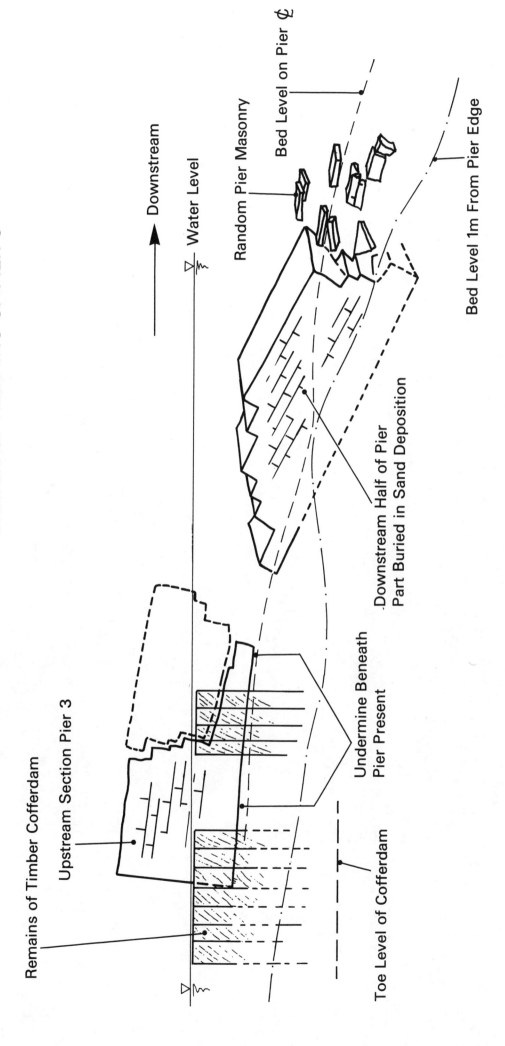

Downstream

Water Level

Random Pier Masonry

Bed Level on Pier ₵

Bed Level 1m From Pier Edge

Downstream Half of Pier
Part Buried in Sand Deposition

Remains of Timber Cofferdam

Upstream Section Pier 3

Undermine Beneath
Pier Present

Toe Level of Cofferdam

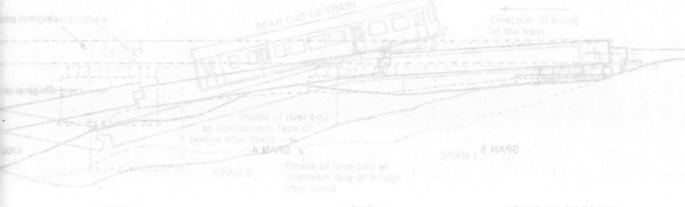
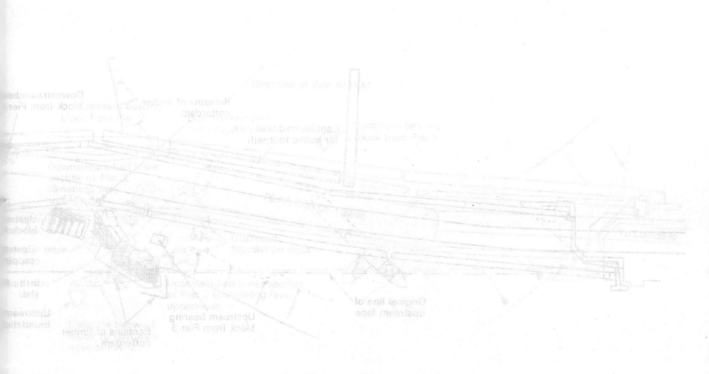